·EXPLORING·

SCIENCE AND MEDICAL DISCOVERIES

**Other books in the
Exploring Science and Medical Discoveries series:**

**Antibiotics
Cloning
Vaccines**

EXPLORING
SCIENCE AND MEDICAL DISCOVERIES

Gene Therapy

Clay Farris Naff, *Book Editor*

Bruce Glassman, *Vice President*
Bonnie Szumski, *Publisher*
Helen Cothran, *Managing Editor*
David M. Haugen, *Series Editor*

GREENHAVEN PRESS
An imprint of Thomson Gale, a part of The Thomson Corporation

THOMSON
™
GALE

Detroit • New York • San Francisco • San Diego • New Haven, Conn.
Waterville, Maine • London • Munich

THOMSON

GALE

LIBRARY OF CONGRESS CATALOGING-IN-PUBLICATION DATA

Gene therapy / Clay Farris Naff, book editor.
    p. cm. — (Exploring science and medical discoveries)
Includes bibliographical references and index.
    ISBN 0-7377-1967-2 (lib. : alk. paper) — ISBN 0-7377-1968-0 (pbk. : alk. paper)
    1. Gene therapy. I. Naff, Clay Farris. II. Series.
RB155.8.G46172   2005
616'.042—dc22   2003062482

Printed in the United States of America

CONTENTS

Chapter 2: The Road to Success

Most great science and medical discoveries emerge slowly from the work of generations of scientists. In their laboratories, far removed from the public eye, scientists seek cures for human diseases, explore more efficient methods to feed the world's hungry, and develop technologies to improve quality of life. A scientist, trained in the scientific method, may spend his or her entire career doggedly pursuing a goal such as a cure for cancer or the invention of a new drug. In the pursuit of these goals, most scientists are single-minded, rarely thinking about the moral and ethical issues that might arise once their new ideas come into the public view. Indeed, it could be argued that scientific inquiry requires just that type of objectivity.

Moral and ethical assessments of scientific discoveries are quite often made by the unscientific—the public—sometimes for good, sometimes for ill. When a discovery is unveiled to society, intense scrutiny often ensues. The media report on it, politicians debate how it should be regulated, ethicists analyze its impact on society, authors vilify or glorify it, and the public struggles to determine whether the new development is friend or foe. Even without fully understanding the discovery or its potential impact, the public will often demand that further inquiry be stopped. Despite such negative reactions, however, scientists rarely quit their pursuits; they merely find ways around the roadblocks.

Embryonic stem cell research, for example, illustrates this tension between science and public response. Scientists engage in embryonic stem cell research in an effort to treat diseases such as Parkinson's and diabetes that are the result of cellular dysfunction. Embryonic stem cells can be derived from early-stage embryos, or blastocysts, and coaxed to form any kind of human cell or tissue. These can then be used to replace damaged or diseased tissues in those suffering from intractable diseases. Many researchers believe that the use of embryonic stem cells to treat human diseases promises to be one of the most important advancements in medicine.

However, embryonic stem cell experiments are highly controversial in the public sphere. At the center of the tumult is the fact
that in order to create embryonic stem cell lines, human embryos
must be destroyed. Blastocysts often come from fertilized eggs that
are left over from fertility treatments. Critics argue that since blastocysts have the capacity to grow into human beings, they should
be granted the full range of rights given to all humans, including
the right not to be experimented on. These analysts contend, therefore, that destroying embryos is unethical. This argument received
attention in the highest office of the United States. President
George W. Bush agreed with the critics, and in August 2001 he announced that scientists using federal funds to conduct embryonic
stem cell research would be restricted to using existing cell lines.
He argued that limiting research to existing lines would prevent any
new blastocysts from being destroyed for research.

Scientists have criticized Bush's decision, saying that restrict-
ing research to existing cell lines severely limits the number and
types of experiments that can be conducted. Despite this considerable roadblock, however, scientists quickly set to work trying to
figure out a way to continue their valuable research. Unsurpris-
ingly, as the regulatory environment in the United States becomes
restrictive, advancements occur elsewhere. A good example concerns the latest development in the field. On February 12, 2004,
professor Hwang Yoon-Young of Hanyang University in Seoul,
South Korea, announced that he was the first to clone a human
embryo and then extract embryonic stem cells from it. Hwang's
research means that scientists may no longer need to use blastocysts to perform stem cell research. Scientists around the world
extol the achievement as a major step in treating human diseases.

The debate surrounding embryonic stem cell research illustrates
the moral and ethical pressure that the public brings to bear on the
scientific community. However, while nonexperts often criticize
scientists for not considering the potential negative impact of their
work, ironically the public's reaction against such discoveries can
produce harmful results as well. For example, although the outcry
against embryonic stem cell research in the United States has resulted in fewer embryos being destroyed, those with Parkinson's,
such as actor Michael J. Fox, have argued that prohibiting the development of new stem cell lines ultimately will prevent a timely
cure for the disease that is killing Fox and thousands of others.

Greenhaven Press's Exploring Science and Medical Discoveries series explores the public uproar that often follows the disclosure of scientific advances in fields such as stem cell research. Each anthology traces the history of one major scientific or medical discovery, investigates society's reaction to the breakthrough, and explores potential new applications and avenues of research. Primary sources provide readers with eyewitness accounts of crucial moments in the discovery process, and secondary sources offer historical perspectives on the scientific achievement and society's reaction to it. Volumes also contain useful research tools, including an introductory essay providing important context, and an annotated table of contents enabling students to quickly locate selections of interest. A thorough index helps readers locate content easily, a detailed chronology helps students trace the history of the discovery, and an extensive bibliography guides readers interested in pursuing further research.

Greenhaven Press's Exploring Science and Medical Discoveries series provides readers with inspiring accounts of how generations of scientists made the world's great discoveries possible and investigates the tremendous impact those innovations have had on the world.

INTRODUCTION

Gene therapy, much like atomic power before it, has been accompanied onto the world stage by utopian hopes and apocalyptic fears. Some people dream of the end of disease, the enhancement of human abilities, and even the conquest of death. Others fear the unforeseen consequences of tampering with genes, the specter of made-to-order children, and even the destruction of human nature. With few experimental successes to date, however, gene therapy remains in the cradle, its prospects uncertain.

Still, though the high-tech insertion of curative genes into ill people is in its infancy, the manipulation of genes goes back a long way. Throughout premodern history, people, acting with only the dimmest understanding of what they were doing, tinkered with the genomes of a great variety of plants and animals. Breeding, cross-fertilization, and hybridizing produced poodles from wolves, wheat from grass, and mules from donkeys and horses.

Unraveling the Secrets of Heredity

Only in the early twentieth century did a real understanding of heredity begin to dawn. Even then, it took until 1953 for researchers to discover precisely where genes, the mechanisms of heredity, were located. Genes are segments of the world's most famous molecule, DNA. So far as is known, DNA is the only molecule capable of carrying and replicating a vast store of biological information.

On April 2, 1953, scientists Francis Crick and James D. Watson of Cambridge University published a paper on the remarkable arrangement of chemical "bases" in DNA, which bind genes into a double helix, a shape rather like a twisted ladder. The paper, which bore the modest title "A Structure for Deoxyribose Nucleic Acid," opens with a now-famous understatement: "This structure has novel features which are of considerable biological interest."[1]

Less than fifty years later, those interesting features are being used to create a whole new way of treating disease: gene therapy. Scientists have developed technology that allows them to use chemical "scissors" to clip a sample of DNA into segments, extract and replicate valuable genes, and then insert them into other genomes. The practice has revolutionized agriculture, where for example genes that make plants more resistant to pests have been transferred from a bacterium into crops. In medicine, progress has been slower.

Scientists have unraveled the entire human genome and have begun experiments to insert and delete genes in people in the hope of curing disease. Some fortunate participants in medical trials have been cured. Many others have not. In 2003 the federal government's Human Genome Project Information Web site offered a gloomy assessment: "The Food and Drug Administration (FDA) has not yet approved any human gene therapy product for sale. Current gene therapy is experimental and has not proven very successful in clinical trials. Little progress has been made since the first gene therapy clinical trial began in 1990."[2]

Extravagant Hopes and Fears

Although gene therapy has yet to break out of the experimental stage, the media has long been hyping both sides of the story. As early as 1990, *Boston Globe* columnist Ellen Goodman published a column bewailing the imminent rise of so-called designer babies. Nearly a decade later, with gene therapy still in the experimental stage but genetic screening already underway, *Time* magazine told its readers:

> If gene therapy lives up to its promise, parents may someday be able to go beyond weeding out undesirable traits and start actually inserting the genes they want—perhaps even genes that have been crafted in a lab. Before the new millennium is many years old, parents may be going to fertility clinics and picking from a list of options the way car buyers order air conditioning and chrome-alloy wheels.[3]

As the twenty-first century unfolded, a reaction set in. Federal regulators suspended then restarted gene therapy experiments. As recently as 2003, a new halt in experiments followed the mysterious appearance of leukemia in some successfully treated children.

Alarmed by deaths during or following gene therapy trials and by concerns over allied biotechnologies such as cloning that offend the moral sensibilities of many, Congress and many state legislatures debated bills that would severely restrict research into all of the new frontiers of human genetic technology.

A Revolution That Will Not Quit

Starry-eyed forecasts and doomsday predictions aside, the genetic revolution appears to be unstoppable. No one country has a monopoly on the tools of biomedical progress. Furthermore, the promise of gene therapy is so great and the needs are so profound that its wholesale abandonment seems a remote possibility. In-

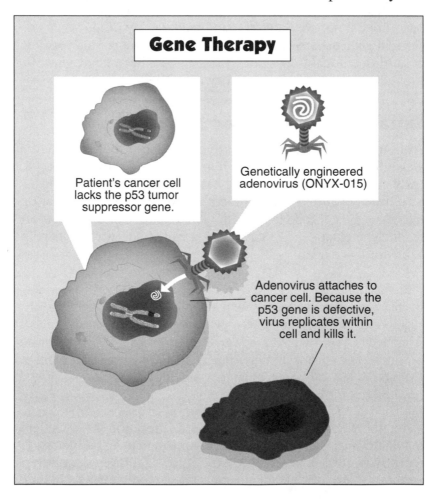

Gene Therapy

Patient's cancer cell lacks the p53 tumor suppressor gene.

Genetically engineered adenovirus (ONYX-015)

Adenovirus attaches to cancer cell. Because the p53 gene is defective, virus replicates within cell and kills it.

deed, a handful of positive results has lent fresh momentum to the effort. "Five years ago, there were no successful gene therapies," British immunologist Bobby Gaspar told a London-based newspaper in 2003. "Now, we have cures."[4]

Cures will likely remain unavailable to the general public, however, until regulators are convinced they are safe and effective. Only in China has a gene therapy regime been approved for clinical treatment. All the same, promising results in treating such long-standing threats to human health as cancer, heart disease, and immune system disorders will almost certainly keep researchers working at perfecting the new technology. And should they succeed, consumer demand for gene therapy is bound to be strong.

Additional incentive for pursuing gene therapy lies in the need for treatments for emerging cancer threats. The thinning of the earth's protective ozone layer, which scientists blame on industrial refrigerants released into the atmosphere over many decades, is contributing to a rise in global skin cancer rates. While sunscreen lotions may help prevent skin cancer, gene therapy is generally seen as the best hope for a cure. The reason is simple: Some people have far greater ability to ward off sun damage than others. Among them are sub-Saharan Africans, South Asian Indians, and Australian aborigines. Gene therapy opens the way to exchange useful genes among groups of people, including, in principle, genes for skin color. The genes from an African, for example, could be inserted into a Swedish woman to make her more resistant to skin cancer. Such a procedure, however, remains a speculative, over-the-horizon solution to a gradually accumulating threat.

Other needs for gene therapy are closer at hand. With their unprecedented global mobility, people using modern transport are unwittingly assisting formerly obscure viral diseases in becoming worldwide outbreaks. The sudden appearance of SARS in the spring of 2003 brought scientists' worst fears into sharp focus: The deadly virus spread in a matter of weeks from southern China to North America, clustering in the Canadian metropolis of Toronto. Only the ancient tool of quarantine succeeded in stamping out the epidemic. Still, epidemiologists predict that the virus that causes SARS will return, and already labs are turning to gene therapy as a way to beat it back. Scientists have identified a genetic variation in some people that appears to render them immune to SARS. If this gene can be added to the genome of vulnerable people, scientists hope they may be able to prevent a new epidemic.

High Hopes in the Scientific Community

Indeed, a consensus appears to be forming among medical researchers that gene therapy has unmatched potential for developing new cures. In part this is because gene therapy can in principle mobilize and augment the body's own defenses. Moreover, because it can transfer genes from one person to another, gene therapy can in principle allow researchers to capitalize on naturally arising immunities rather than having to invent new treatments from scratch. By conveying the evolutionary successes of even a few individuals in, for example, resisting AIDS to others who lack that genetic fortune, gene therapy may prove a great boon indeed.

Additionally, gene therapy's cures can be passed down to future generations, breaking chains of suffering that have plagued certain families and communities throughout history. For example, so-called germ line gene therapy—altering the genomes that go into sperm or eggs—could spell the end of such hereditary diseases as cystic fibrosis, sickle-cell anemia, and Tay-Sachs. However, no one has attempted such cures because germ line therapy is deeply controversial. Its multigenerational aspect leads many people to question the assurances offered by supporters of gene therapy. Not only are there widespread concerns about the abuse of such therapies to create designer babies, but many people find the idea of changing a genome for all descendants in a particular line repugnant. At present, federal guidelines for gene therapy research rule out any proposal that involves alteration of the germ line.

Formidable Challenges

Despite high hopes, many challenges remain for those working in the gene therapy field. The biggest obstacle to the success of gene therapy is that knowledge of genetics, the science underlying gene therapy, remains far from complete. Although the map of human genes has been drawn, the dynamic interactions of genes remain largely mysterious.

Scientists in the field are increasingly aware that few genes operate in isolation. The idea that there is a single gene for every human trait has been discarded. Instead, scientists recognize that most genes work in shifting coalitions that have immensely complicated and entangled arrays of effects. This means that replacing one gene with another can have many unforeseen consequences alongside

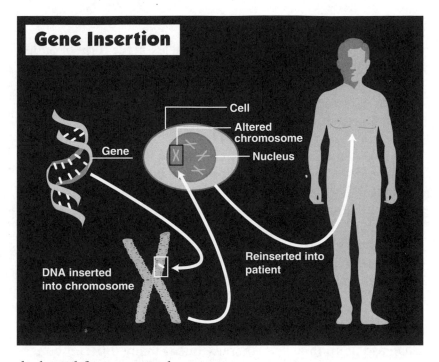

Gene Insertion

Cell

Altered chromosome

Gene

Nucleus

DNA inserted into chromosome

Reinserted into patient

the hoped-for cure or enhancement.

Gene therapy faces additional challenges before it can become a regular weapon in the medical armament. Most of the attempts to insert therapeutic genes into patients have involved viruses as the delivery agent, or vector. Typically, scientists will weaken a virus before employing it as a vector. However, viruses have billions of years of experience at promoting their own interests at the expense of their hosts. At least two problems have arisen. Even weakened viruses can trigger a massive immune response in some people, often to the patient's detriment. Also, viruses often refuse to stay put at the treatment site, instead migrating and replicating throughout the patient's body.

In January 2003 the FDA announced that it was placing a hold on "all active gene therapy trials using retroviral vectors to insert genes into blood stem cells." The federal regulatory agency said it took the action after learning "that a second child treated in a French gene therapy trial has developed a leukemia-like condition."[5] Although some trials later resumed, concerns that tame viruses might not be as innocuous as thought continue to haunt researchers. Work on alternatives continues, but it remains unclear whether a truly safe and reliable method of gene delivery can be devised.

Apocalyptic Fears

Gene therapy also faces enormous obstacles in the form of public fears. Although nothing remotely like a designer baby is at present possible, genetic screening has already made it possible for parents in some Asian countries to selectively abort female fetuses in favor of male ones, causing a noticeable gender imbalance in the populations of countries such as India, China, and South Korea. This development has caused some people to fear that gene therapy may lead to many other dangerous imbalances in society. For example, if the wealthy gain a monopoly on technologies that make their children smarter, stronger, or otherwise superior, some critics say egalitarianism, the foundation of democracy, will collapse.

Still others worry that if gene therapy opens up a whole new suite of treatments to the public, it will accelerate the already alarming trend toward unsustainable cost inflation in the health care system. No one knows how expensive gene therapy might prove, but history suggests that health care does not become cheaper with new discoveries.

On top of all this, gene therapy raises many difficult ethical questions. Many wonder if it is right to tamper with an embryo without the consent of the person who will develop from it. Others question who should decide if a child is to get gene therapy. Still others ask where the line between a cure and an enhancement should be drawn.

Global Effort Underway

These questions and many others demand answers, but it may not be possible to wait until consensus about gene therapy emerges in America. Gene therapy is moving ahead. Late in 2003, China became the first country to approve gene therapy for general use in the fight against cancer. More than six hundred gene therapy trials with human subjects are underway at this writing, spread across twenty countries as distant and different from each other as Egypt, Singapore, and Sweden. While the majority of gene therapy research continues to be conducted in the United States, recent history suggests that more countries will take the plunge and that multinational corporations will play a significant role in shaping the development and use of gene therapy.

It may not matter, for example, what kinds of protections and restrictions the U.S. government puts on experiments if biotech companies seek volunteers for gene therapy trials in poor countries where regulations are lax and enforcement is loose. It may not matter what kind of prohibitions are enacted against germ line therapy if the wealthy are able to send their children abroad for "enhancements." With gene therapy developing on a global stage, it may simply be impossible for the United States or any other government to slow it in response to public concerns.

On the other hand, the worst fears about gene therapy may prove to be unfounded. The idea of enhancing people is a far cry from curing a specific disease. Research offers broad grounds for hope that gene therapy will eventually play a key role in defeating cancer, curing hereditary diseases, and staving off many of the ravages of old age. Beyond this, however, it is quite unclear whether genes can ever be manipulated to enhance memory, intelligence, or other more generalized traits, especially if concerns about side effects are taken into account. "I think it's very unlikely that tinkering with one gene is going to increase intelligence and do nothing else," says Tim Bliss, head of neurophysiology at the National Institute for Medical Research in London. "In my view talk of genetically enhancing human intelligence is nonsense."[6]

Too Big to Ignore

Whether welcome or not, gene therapy is likely to make an enormous impact on society. For the generation now reaching young adulthood, gene therapy may become a major component of health care during their lifetimes. It may do what a generation of drug research has failed to do: cure the scourge of cancer. It may put an end to the grief and horror of parents who discover that their children have been born with a fatal genetic disorder such as Huntington's disease. It may prove to be the magic bullet that halts the global spread of AIDS. It may even extend the average life span beyond the century mark and add to old age the quality of life enjoyed by the young.

As one of the founders of the field, surgeon W. French Anderson, has remarked:

> The field of gene therapy has been criticized for promising too much and providing too little during its first 10 years of existence. But gene therapy, like every other major new technology, takes

time to develop. . . . Gene therapy will succeed with time. And it is important that it does succeed, because no other area of medicine holds as much promise for providing cures for the many devastating diseases that now ravage humankind.[7]

It may do all of this and more—for those individuals and nations that can afford it. Gene therapy will raise profound policy questions for every member of society, questions about who has access, who decides, who pays, and how much health care a society can afford. Moreover, it will be no respecter of national boundaries. In an age of rapid globalization, gene therapy is likely to be the first major technology to be simultaneously developed in many countries. At the same time, however, because of its controversial aspects it is likely to make international cooperation and consensus more difficult to achieve. That will be all the more true if gene therapy moves beyond the mere curing of disease and into uncharted waters of human enhancement. Whether utopian hopes or apocalyptic fears about gene therapy come to pass will depend largely on how people around the world respond to these challenges.

Notes

1. Francis Crick and James D. Watson, "A Structure for Deoxyribose Nucleic Acid," *Nature*, April 2, 1953.
2. U.S. Department of Energy Office of Science, Office of Biological and Environmental Research, Human Genome Program, Human Genome Information Project, www.ornl.gov.
3. Michael D. Lemonick, "The Future of Medicine: Designer Babies: Parents Can Now Pick a Kid's Sex and Screen for Genetic Illness. Will They Someday Select for Brains and Beauty Too?" *Time*, January 11, 1999.
4. Quoted in Charles Arthur, "Doctors Struggle with the Ethical Dilemma of Gene Therapy; Despite Controversy and Setbacks, the Pioneering Treatments for Congenital Disorders Remains a Prime Goal of Medical Researchers," *Independent*, October 4, 2002.
5. U.S. Food and Drug Administration, "FDA Places Temporary Halt on Gene Therapy Trials Using Retroviral Vectors in Blood Stem Cells," FDA Talk Paper, January 14, 2003, www.fda.gov.
6. Tim Bliss, "Genetic Engineering Boosts Intelligence," BBC News, September 1, 1999, http://news.bbc.co.uk.
7. W. French Anderson, "Gene Therapy: The Best of Times, the Worst of Times," *Science*, April 28, 2000.

CHAPTER 1

Understanding and Manipulating Genes

Understanding Heredity

By George W. Burns

According to George W. Burns in the following selection, excerpted from his book *The Science of Genetics: An Introduction to Heredity*, people have long observed that offspring tend to resemble their parents. The ancients puzzled over the process responsible for the transmission of traits but lacked both the microscopes and the methods to arrive at reliable answers. Indeed, some cultures seem to have missed the connection between sex and pregnancy, and others devised many naive theories to explain what is now called heredity. Even the most scientifically oriented societies failed to grasp the means by which characteristics are passed on. Burns explains that it was not until an Augustinian monk named Gregor Mendel identified genes through breeding peas that a true understanding of heredity dawned. Using quickly reproducing organisms such as mice, scientists thereafter began to devise experiments in which to study how genes direct inheritance. This early research eventually led to the discovery of DNA and the advent of gene therapy. The late George W. Burns was a biologist at Ohio Wesleyan University.

Certainly one of the most exciting fields of biological science, if not of all science, is genetics. This is the study of the mechanisms of heredity by which traits or characteristics are passed from generation to generation. Not only has modern genetics had a compact history, being essentially a product of the twentieth century, but it has made almost explosive progress from the rediscovery in 1900 of Mendel's basic observations of the 1860s to a fairly full comprehension of underlying principles at the molecular level. As our knowledge of these operating mechanisms developed, it became apparent that they are remarkably similar in their fundamental behavior for all kinds of organisms, whether man or mouse, bacterium or corn. But geneticists' quest for truth and understanding is far from completed; as in other sciences, the answer to one question raises new ones and opens whole new avenues of inquiry.

Genetics is personally relevant to everyone. Man is a genetic animal; each of us is the product of a long series of matings. People differ among themselves with regard to the expression of many traits; one has some inherited characteristics of his father and certain ones of his mother, but often, as well, some not exhibited by either parent. Familiar examples abound in persons of your own acquaintance—hair or eye color, curly or straight hair, height, intelligence, and baldness, to list but a few. Less obvious genetic traits include such diverse ones as form of ear lobes, ability to roll the tongue, ability to taste the chemical phenylthiocarbamide (PTC), red-green color blindness, hemophilia (or "bleeder's disease") extra fingers or toes, or ability to produce insulin (lack of which results in diabetes). Note that some of these characteristics seem purely morphological, being concerned primarily with form and structure, whereas others are clearly physiological. Look about you at your friends and family for points of difference or similarity. Many of these characteristics have genetic bases. . . .

An Ancient Fascination

It is well established that as much as six thousand years ago [man] kept records of pedigrees of such domestic animals as the horse or of crop plants like rice. Because certain animals and plants were necessary for his survival and culture, man has, since the beginning of recorded history at least, attempted to develop improved varieties. But the story of man's concern with heredity during his lifetime on this planet has been, until recently, one of interest largely in results rather than in fundamental understanding of the mechanisms involved.

As one examines the development of ideas relating to these mechanisms, he finds the way replete with misconceptions, many of them naïve in the light of modern knowledge. These theories may be divided roughly into three categories: (1) *"vapors and fluids,"* (2) *preformation*, and (3) *particulate.* Such early Greek philosophers as Pythagoras (500 B.C.) proposed that "vapors" derived from various organs unite to form a new individual. Then

Aristotle assigned a "vitalizing" effect to semen, which, he suggested, was highly purified blood, a notion that was to influence thinking for almost two thousand years.

By the seventeenth century sperm and egg had been discovered, and the Dutch scientist [Jan] Swammerdam theorized that sex cells contained miniatures of the adult. Literature of that time contains drawings of models or manikins within sperm heads which imaginative workers reported seeing. Such theories of preformation persisted well into the eighteenth century, by which time the German investigator Wolff offered experimental evidence that no preformed embryo existed in the egg of the chicken.

But [Pierre De] Maupertuis in France, recognizing that preformation could not easily account for transmission of traits to the offspring from both parents, had proposed in the early 1800s that minute particles, one from each body part, united in sexual reproduction to form a new individual. In some instances, he reasoned, particles from the male parent might dominate those from the female, and in other cases the reverse might be true. Thus the notion of particulate inheritance came into consideration. Maupertuis was actually closer to the truth, in general terms, than anyone realized for more than a century.

Darwin's Wrong Guess

Charles Darwin suggested, in the nineteenth century, essentially the same basic mechanism in his theory of pangenesis, the central idea of which had first been put forward by Hippocrates (400 B.C.). Under this concept, each part of the body produced minute particles ("gemmules") which were contained in the blood of the entire body but eventually concentrated in the reproductive organs. Thus, an individual would represent a "blending" of both parents. Moreover, acquired characters would be inherited because, as parts of the body changed, so did the pangenes they produced. A champion weight lifter, therefore, should produce children with strong arm muscles; such transmission of acquired traits we know does not occur.

Pangenesis was disproved later in the same century by the German biologist [August] Weismann. In a well-known experiment he cut off the tails of mice for twenty-two generations, yet each new lot of offspring consisted only of animals with tails. If the source of pangenes for tails was removed, how, he reasoned, could the next generation have tails? Yet, in spite of these early problems with the idea of particulate inheritance, its basic concept is the central core of our modern understanding.

Most attempts to explain observed breeding results failed because investigators generally tried to encompass simultaneously *all* variations, whether heritable or not. Nor was the progress of scientific thought or the development of suitable equipment and techniques ready to help point the way. It was the Augustinian monk Gregor Mendel who laid the groundwork for our modern concept of the particulate theory. He did so by attacking the problem in logical fashion, concentrating on one or a few observable, contrasting traits in a controlled breeding program. Both by his method and by his suggestion of causal "factors" (which we now call *genes*) Mendel came closer to a real understanding of heredity than had anyone in the preceding five thousand years or more, yet he only opened the door for others. An understanding of the cellular mechanisms was still to be developed. . . .

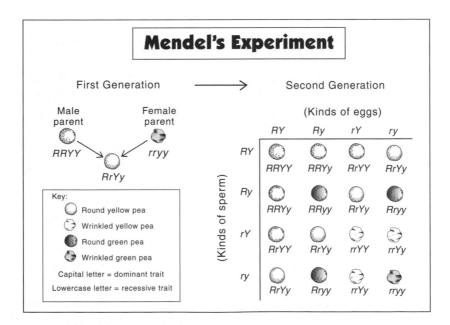

How to Plan a Genetic Experiment

There are six important considerations for choosing a plant or animal for genetic experiments:

1. *Variation.* The organism chosen should show a number of de-

tectable differences. Nothing could be learned of the inheritance of skin color in man, for example, if all human beings were alike in this respect. In general, the larger the number of discontinuous traits and the more clearly marked they are, the greater the usefulness of the species for genetic study.

2. *Recombination.* Genetic analysis of a species is greatly expedited if it has some effective means of combining, in one individual, traits of two parents. Such *recombination* permits comparison of one expression of a character with another expression of the same trait (e.g., tall versus dwarf *size*, brown versus blue *eye color*) through several generations. In many organisms recombination occurs as the result of *sexual reproduction*, in which two sex cells (gametes), generally from two different parents, combine as a fertilized egg (zygote). The sexual process is characteristic of higher animals and plants, and occurs in many lower forms as well. In viruses and bacteria there occur parasexual processes which also bring about recombination. . . .

On the other hand, many organisms reproduce *asexually* or *vegetatively* and cannot furnish recombinational information. Basically, asexual reproduction may involve specialized cells (often called *spores*), daughter cells (in unicellular forms), parts of a single parent (cuttings, grafts, fragmentation, etc.), or parthonogenesis, in which an individual develops from an unfertilized egg, as in the male honeybee. By and large, a means of recombination is required for genetic study.

3. *Controlled matings.* Systematic study of an organism's genetics is far easier if we can make controlled matings, choosing parental lines with particular purposes in mind, and keep careful records of offspring through several generations. The mouse, fruit fly, corn, and the red bread mold (*Neurospora*), for instance, make better genetic subjects in this respect than does man. In human genetics we are dependent largely on pedigree analysis, or studies of traits as they have appeared in a given family line for several past generations. Although such analyses are certainly useful, the human geneticist must rely largely on lines of progeny that *have been* established and cannot devise desired crosses of his own.

4. *Short life cycle.* Acquisition of genetic knowledge is facilitated if the organism chosen requires only a short time between generations. Mice, which are sexually mature at 5 or 6 weeks of age and have a gestation period of about 19 to 31 days, are much more useful, for instance, than elephants, which mature in 8 to 16

years and have a gestation period of nearly 2 years. Likewise, the fruit fly, *Drosophila*, is much used in investigations because it may provide as many as five or six generations in a season. But first place for short life cycle goes to bacteria and to bacteriophages (or simply phages, viruses that infect bacteria), which, under optimum conditions, have a generation time of only 20 minutes! Both bacteria and phages also offer a number of other advantages for genetic study.

5. *Large number of offspring.* Genetic studies are greatly speeded if the organism chosen produces fairly sizable lots of progeny per mating. Cattle, with generally one calf per breeding, do not provide nearly as much information in a given time as many lower forms of life where offspring may number many thousands.

6. *Convenience of handling.* For practical reasons, an experimental species should be of a type that can be raised and maintained conveniently and relatively inexpensively. Whales are obviously less useful in this context than are bacteria! . . .

Solving the Puzzles

After an initial and appropriate preoccupation with descriptive genetics, scientists turned naturally to problems of the mechanics of the processes they observed. The "what" of the earliest twentieth century rapidly gave way to a concern with "how." Parallels between inheritance patterns and the structure and behavior of cells were noted by a number of pioneer investigators. Thus, *cytology* [the study of cells] rapidly became an important adjunct to genetics. In fact, a pair of papers by [Walter] Sutton as early as 1902 and 1903 clearly pointed the way to a physical basis for the burgeoning science of heredity. Sutton concluded his 1902 paper with a bold prediction: "I may finally call attention to the probability that (the behavior of chromosomes) may constitute the physical basis of the Mendelian law of heredity." Truly the door was thereby opened to an objective examination of the physical mechanisms of the genetic processes.

As the science of genetics developed rapidly during the first quarter of [the twentieth] century, a considerable body of knowledge was built up for such organisms as *Drosophila*, corn, the laboratory mouse, and tomato concerning *what* traits are inherited and how different expressions of these are related to each other. Genetic maps, based on breeding experiments, were constructed for these and other species showing relative distances between genes on their chromosomes. Geneticists began to turn from concern with inheritance patterns of such traits as eye color in fruit flies to problems of *how* the observable trait is produced. Especially in the period since the beginning of World War II, a central question has been the *structure* of the gene and the mode of its operation. As the search for answers has proceeded ever more deeply into molecular levels, an increasingly important part in genetic study has been played by chemistry and physics. Contributions of these sciences have been such as to enable geneticists to gain a clear concept of the molecular nature of the gene and its operation.

From Discovery to Practical Application

Genetics appeals to many of us not only because we are parts of an ongoing genetic stream but also because it has had such an exciting history in which theory has evolved out of observation and led, in turn, to experimental proof of fundamental operating mechanisms. Of course, any science may make the same claim, but the history of man's knowledge and understanding of genetics is to other sciences as a time-lapse movie of a growth process is to a normal-speed film. A fraction of a century ago the scientific community at large knew nothing of genetic mechanisms. Now, however, we can, with considerable accuracy, even construct molecular models of genes, atom by atom. But besides being a fascinating intellectual discipline intimately related to ourselves, genetics has many important practical applications. Some of these are fairly familiar; others may be less so.

The history of improvement of food crops and domestic animals by selective breeding is too well known to warrant detailed description here. Increases in yield of crops like corn and rice, improvement in flavor and size, as well as the production of seedless varieties of fruits, and advances in meat production of cattle and swine have markedly benefited mankind. As the population of the world continues to increase, this practical utilization of genetics is likely to assume even greater significance. The problem of breeding disease-resistant plants is likewise a never ending one.

Applications of genetics in the general field of medicine are numerous and growing. Many diseases and abnormalities are now known to have genetic bases. Hemophilia, some types of diabetes, an anemia known as hemolytic icterus, some forms of deafness and of blindness, several hemoglobin abnormalities, and Rh incompatibility are a few conditions that fall into this category. Recognition of their inherited nature is important in anticipating their possible future occurrence in a given family, so that appropriate preventive steps may be taken.

Closely related is the whole field of genetic counseling. Some estimate of the likelihood of a particular desirable or undesirable trait appearing in the children of a given couple can be provided by one who has sound genetic training and some information on the ancestors of the prospective parents. Questions encountered might range from the probability of a couple's having any red-haired children to the chance of muscular dystrophy appearing in the offspring.

Genetics has its legal applications, too. Analysis of blood type, a genetically determined character, may be used to solve problems of disputed parentage. Questions of baby mixups in hospitals, illegitimate children, and estate claims can often be clarified by genetics. . . .

Our quest for the "why" and "how" of genetics will grow ever more specific until we are able to answer on the deepest molecular levels yet penetrated by science. In the process we should not only acquire some fundamental genetic knowledge about ourselves, but also sharpen our powers of critical, analytical, skeptical thinking.

From the Discovery of Genes to the Mapping of Genomes

By Dinshaw Dadachanji

Charles Darwin, a keen observer of nature, gained lasting fame for his theory of evolution, first published in his 1859 book, *On the Origin of Species.* Central to his theory was the idea that offspring resemble their parents, but not precisely. However, Darwin never figured out exactly how the inheritance and variation took place. According to Dinshaw Dadachanji in the following selection, even as Darwin was elaborating his theory, a solitary researcher in central Europe was discovering the nature of heredity. Gregor Mendel proposed that invisible units of heredity (later called genes) were the vehicles by which traits passed from parent to offspring. Dadachanji explains that the work of Gregor Mendel went unnoticed until the next century but is still recognized as one of the key steps to understanding genetics. In the twentieth century scientists discovered that genes are made of long strands of DNA arranged in loops called chromosomes. Once scientists understood the structures responsible for heredity, they then began to explore how the process of heredity works. Beginning in 1986, research teams around the world began to map the human genome, the sum of all genes that compose the recipe for a person. Dadachanji reports that intense competition between the teams facilitated advances. By 2001, two teams reported that they had mapped 95 percent of the human genome. This important work is expected to help doctors devise early diagnostic tests for genetic diseases and aid in the design of new drugs and gene therapies. Dadachanji is science editor for the *World & I* magazine.

I magine transporting yourself to the mid–nineteenth century and arriving in the serene garden of an Augustinian monastery in the city of Brünn (now Brno in the Czech Republic). Your gaze is drawn to a monk who is meticulously tending rows of pea plants. You notice that some plants are tall, others are short; some have purple flowers, others, white. Every so often, the monk opens the pods and examines the peas. Some peas are round, others are wrinkled; some are green, others are yellow. The monk is engrossed in his work and takes copious notes. But you fail to grasp much significance here. What does it all mean?

Returning to our current era, you dash off to a library, flip through a scientific text, and find his picture. He is identified as Gregor Mendel. You learn that after eight years of experimentation with tens of thousands of pea plants, he had arrived at a set of principles explaining how inherited traits are transmitted during sexual reproduction. But the significance of his work, published in 1866, went unrecognized until it was rediscovered in 1900. Over time, it became clear that Mendel had begun laying the foundations of modern genetics.

Mendel had realized that visible, inherited traits are manifestations of discrete though invisible units of heredity. In 1909, Danish botanist Wilhelm Johannsen proposed that each unit of heredity could be called a gene (from the Greek word *genos*, meaning birth). Later, the entire complement of genes in an organism was given the name genome.

The Gene Emerges

During the first half of the twentieth century, a number of fundamental characteristics of genes were discovered. In particular, it became clear that (a) genes are located on chromosomes and are arranged in linear fashion; (b) each gene contains instructions for the production of a protein (or protein subunit); and (c) genes are constituted of a cellular substance called DNA (deoxyribonucleic acid).

It was further learned that DNA occurs in long chains composed of building blocks, called nucleotides, each of which has three parts: a sugar (deoxyribose), a phosphate, and a base. Four types of nucleotides were found, each possessing one of four bases: adenine (A), thymine (T), guanine (G), and cytosine (C). Each DNA sample was found to contain nearly equal amounts of A and T and nearly equal amounts of G and C. Moreover, X-ray diffraction patterns suggested that DNA is a symmetrical, helical molecule with certain dimensions.

Armed with this information, Francis Crick and James Watson began working on the three-dimensional structure of DNA. In a landmark paper published in 1953, they described DNA as a double helix, in which alternating sugar and phosphate groups formed the backbones of the two strands, while the bases on opposite strands pointed toward each other and were paired—A with T, G with C. Thereafter, DNA length was measured in terms of its number of base pairs (bp). Five years later, Matthew Meselson and Franklin Stahl showed that DNA is replicated in such a way that each strand in a parent molecule acts as a template on which a new, complementary, strand is synthesized.

Then in 1961, Sydney Brenner, François Jacob, and Jacques Monod found a type of RNA (ribonucleic acid) that carried information encoded in DNA to the site of protein synthesis. It was called messenger RNA (mRNA). After several years of experimentation, teams led by Har Gobind Khorana, Marshall Nirenberg, and Severo Ochoa showed that each amino acid in a protein is specified by a particular triplet (codon) of nucleotides in mRNA.

RNA Comes into Focus

Meanwhile, other experiments distinguished mRNA from two additional types: transfer RNA, which carries amino acids to the site of protein synthesis; and ribosomal RNA, which occurs in the "workbenches" (ribosomes) on which proteins are made. The synthesis of RNA from a DNA template was called transcription; the synthesis of a protein from an RNA template was called translation; and both processes were referred to as gene expression.

Later, researchers studying the genes of animal viruses and eukaryotic cells discovered that a gene can be "interrupted" by segments that are not represented in the corresponding mRNA, so these segments do not code for the protein product. These noncoding regions were called introns; the coding regions, exons. Further experiments showed that a gene is first copied to form a long precursor RNA, which then undergoes cutting (to remove the introns) and splicing together of the exons to produce the final mRNA.

Around 1970, Hamilton Smith and other researchers discovered "restriction" enzymes that could cut DNA at specific sites. Soon, Paul Berg pioneered the use of these molecular scissors to produce "recombinant" DNA, by cutting DNA segments from different species and sticking them together in desired fashion.

Extending this approach, Herbert Boyer and Stanley Cohen showed in 1973 how a gene could be removed from animal DNA and transferred to bacterial cells, where it was copied and produced the corresponding animal protein. This technology to clone a gene—that is, to produce exact copies of a gene in a foreign host—gave birth to the genetic engineering industry.

In 1977, two research teams—Frederick Sanger's group and Walter Gilbert and Allan Maxam—announced new techniques for the rapid sequencing of nucleotides in DNA. These methods allowed researchers to obtain the sequences of genes and viral DNA, several thousand base pairs in length. Sanger's method was later modified and incorporated into automated sequencing machines.

Tackling the Human Genome

Around 1985, the idea of sequencing the whole human genome was being discussed, but it met with much skepticism. The enormous size of the human genome—about 3 billion base pairs in 24 types of chromosomes—and the huge anticipated cost seemed prohibitive.

[By] 1986, a conference convened by Charles DeLisi and David Smith of the Department of Energy (DOE) endorsed what was called the Human Genome Initiative and pilot projects were begun. Two years later, the National Research Council (NRC) released a report advocating a 15-year program that would begin by mapping human chromosomes and finding the sequences of simpler genomes before moving to large-scale sequencing of human DNA.

The tide had begun to turn. Some argued that the human genome was our "thread of life" or even "book of life," and that by determining the entire sequence we would discover more about ourselves. Others emphasized that the sequence would help us find the causes of and treatments for numerous genetic diseases.

In September 1988, James Wyngaarden, then-director of the

National Institutes of Health (NIH), established the Office of Human Genome Research and appointed Watson to lead it. The NIH and DOE then agreed to collaborate on what became known as the Human Genome Project (HGP). The NIH office was upgraded a year later to become the National Center for Human Genome Research (NCHGR). And in 1990, the NIH and DOE presented Congress with a five-year plan as the first phase of their 15-year project, with an overall price tag of $3 billion. October 1 of that year was designated as the official starting date.

In April 1992, however, Watson resigned from the NCHGR, displeased that the NIH had been filing for patents on thousands of partial genes whose functions were mostly unknown. Those DNA sequences were being identified by J. Craig Venter and others at the NIH, using a new method involving what were called expressed sequence tags. Soon, Venter left the NIH and founded a nonprofit group—the Institute for Genomic Research (TIGR)—to continue his gene-identification approach and market his discoveries through a sister company. Watson's place was taken by Francis Collins in 1993.

International participation in the genome project came early on, with efforts coordinated through the Human Genome Organization, founded in 1988. In 1993, Britain's Wellcome Trust and the Medical Research Council established the Sanger Centre for large-scale genome sequencing. Other research centers that joined the project were located in France, Japan, Germany, and China. At a 1996 meeting in Bermuda, the partners agreed to make their sequencing information available in public databases within 24 hours of generation.

A Modest Milestone

The first complete genome sequence of a free-living organism—the bacterium *Haemophilus influenzae*—was published in May 1995. It was a collaborative effort between Venter's group and Hamilton Smith's team, using a strategy called "whole-genome shotgun sequencing". Over the next few years, the DNA sequences of other small organisms were published by HGP researchers as well as Venter and his collaborators. These included the genome sequences of yeast (*Saccharomyces cerevisiae*), bacteria (*Escherichia coli* and others), and a worm (*Caenorhabditis elegans*).

In January 1997, the NCHGR was elevated to become the National Human Genome Research Institute (NHGRI), and the DOE established the Joint Genome Institute. Then in May 1998, Venter made the startling announcement that he was starting a new business—later named Celera Genomics—that would produce the complete human genome sequence in three years for just $300 million. He planned to follow the whole-genome shotgun strategy, using 300 of the latest automated capillary sequencing instruments coupled with supercomputing technology.

In response, the NIH and DOE announced new goals in September 1998: The HGP would have a "working draft" ready by 2001, followed by the finished genome sequence in 2003. Six months later, the first deadline was moved to spring 2000. But the HGP partners remained committed to the slower, more methodical approach known as "hierarchical shotgun sequencing".

Soon thereafter, Venter's group and collaborators in Berkeley produced the genome sequence of the fruit fly *Drosophila melanogaster.* The 180-megabase sequence, published in March 2000, was the largest genome yet completed, and this project's success was taken to validate the whole-genome shotgun strategy.

As the race to complete the human genome sequence heated up, the two sides began to feud. But thanks to the mediation of Ari Patrinos, current director of the DOE Office of Biological and Environmental Research, they agreed to announce their working drafts simultaneously. That joint announcement came on June 26, 2000, hosted by President [Bill] Clinton at the White House.

Eventually, analyses of the draft sequences were published at practically the same time but in separate journals. The results of the international partners—20 research groups—were reported in the February 15, 2001, issue of *Nature*, while Celera's work appeared in the February 16, 2001, issue of *Science.* These results, coupled with those obtained from earlier studies, cover about 95 percent of the human genome.

A Surprising Shortfall in Genes

Perhaps the biggest surprise to emerge from these sequencing studies is in terms of the total number of genes, with estimates ranging from 25,000 to 40,000. These numbers fall dramatically short of earlier predictions of finding 80,000–100,000 genes. By comparison, the mustard weed has about 25,000 genes, the worm has roughly 20,000, the fruit fly has 14,000, and yeast has 6,000.

How, then, does a relatively small leap in the number of genes endow humans with far greater complexity than these other creatures? One explanation is that the RNA made from each gene can be spliced in alternative ways, producing several mRNAs that are translated into different proteins. The human body is thought to contain about 95,000 different types of proteins, so it would appear that, on average, each gene codes for three proteins. Another possibility is that genes expressed at low levels may have been missed by certain methods used.

Whatever the case, it appears that the RNA-coding regions amount to about 28 percent of the genome, while the protein-coding sequences correspond to only about 1.4 percent of the genome. Some noncoding sequences probably contain signals that regulate gene expression, but the functions of other noncoding regions are unknown, so they are often labeled "junk" DNA.

In the DNA sequence of each chromosome, some areas are rich in G and C nucleotides, others are rich in A and T. It appears that 50 percent or more of the genes occur as clumps in the GC-rich regions. These gene clumps are generally flanked by long repeats of the dinucleotide CG, which may assist in regulating gene expression. By contrast, most of the noncoding stretches of DNA occur in AT-rich regions.

The human genome encodes a more complex collection of proteins than the proteins found in invertebrates [such as shellfish, for example]. This complexity is achieved partly by the presence of protein-coding sequences that are unique to vertebrates but even more by the rearrangement of protein-coding domains present in earlier species. Also, many genes have been duplicated to produce large protein families.

HGP researchers found that over 200 human genes are closely related in sequence to certain bacterial genes, although similar sequences are missing in invertebrates such as the fruit fly and worm. It was suggested, therefore, that bacterial DNA may have been directly transferred to the chromosomal DNA of an early vertebrate ancestor of humans, perhaps during bacterial infections. This interpretation has been hotly disputed by two research teams—one at TIGR, the other at GlaxoSmithKline—that looked at additional data and offered alternative interpretations.

As much as 50 percent of the human genome consists of repeated sequences, ranging in size from a few bases to large DNA segments. Most of the repeats occur in AT-rich regions, and their functional significance is unknown. But some, which lie in the GC-rich (and gene-rich) regions, may play a useful role. In addition, large repeated segments that occur at chromosomal ends (telomeres) and constrictions (centromeres) may be important in maintaining the chromosome's structural integrity.

By comparison, repeat elements occupy just 3 percent of the fruit fly's genome and 7 percent of the worm's genome. Their phenomenal accumulation in the amoeba explains why its genome is 200-fold larger than ours.

It appears that over the course of evolutionary history, the repeat elements have jumped around and rearranged their corresponding genome, producing new genes and modifying existing ones. Some repeats (called SINE and LINE elements) in human chromosomes still seem active, others (LTR retroposons) are nearly inactive, and yet others (DNA transposons) are totally inactive. Some sequence repeats appear to stretch back 800 million years.

In 1999, an international consortium was formed to identify and map single-nucleotide polymorphisms (SNPs)—that is, single-nucleotide variations in the genomic sequences of individuals. This consortium, working with the genome sequencing partnership, has already catalogued about 1.4 million SNPs, many of which should be helpful in the study of genes linked to diseases.

A comparison of the genomic sequences of various people would show a sequence similarity of about 99.9 percent. The difference of 0.1 percent can help explain the uniqueness of each person's physical traits, and it also provides information about the genetic basis of certain diseases. It should be noted, though, that most genetic differences among us are distributed among people of all ethnicities and races. Thus, these results provide no basis to draw racial boundaries between peoples.

Putting Knowledge to Use

Having published their respective working drafts of the human genome, both HGP and Celera scientists are continuing toward their goal of obtaining a "finished" sequence in which the gaps are closed and there is no more than 1 error per 10,000 bp. The HGP's map-based approach should be particularly useful in resolving ambiguities in areas with repeated sequences. At the same time, researchers are seeking out the precise locations of the coding and noncoding regions and are annotating the DNA accordingly.

Our knowledge of the human genome sequence, coupled with the newly produced genetic and SNP maps, should provide a number of potential benefits, particularly in the area of medicine. For instance, new diagnostic tests can be devised for earlier detection of genetic diseases and predispositions to diseases. The knowledge will also help in the design and production of new types of drugs and therapies. In addition, it will enable scientists to evaluate the risks of exposure to radiation and toxic agents.

DNA sequence data can be of further use in forensics—to help identify both crime suspects and victims and to establish familial relationships. The genome sequences of individuals and SNP maps should also be useful in matching organ donors with recipients.

Knowledge of an individual's genetic makeup also raises serious ethical and social concerns. For instance, how do we safeguard the privacy of genetic information and prevent it from becoming an issue in insurance coverage or employment situations? In anticipation of such concerns, the HGP has devoted about 3 percent of its budget to study the impact of the project in these areas.

The genome project naturally leads to the field called comparative genomics, which involves comparing the human genome sequence with the DNA sequences of other species. This approach should be helpful in determining gene functions, disease mechanisms, and developments in evolutionary history. Recently, both Celera and the HGP announced draft sequences of the mouse genome. This information is especially important, given that mice and humans share similar sets of genes and the mouse is a model organism for the study of human diseases.

A new project being discussed is studying the proteome—the full complement of proteins encoded by the genome; or, in a narrower sense, the set of proteins made in a cell at a given time. The technology for large-scale purification and identification of proteins is still under development, but an international Human Proteome Organization has already been formed. A more readily doable project is studying the transcriptome, the full set of mRNAs transcribed from a genome.

Recently, the DOE proposed another ambitious program, named "Genomes to Life," with the goal of moving from our knowledge of DNA sequences to obtaining a comprehensive perspective on whole biological systems. In light of proposals such as these, observers predict that the twenty-first century will probably be an "era of biology."

Discovering the Structure of DNA

By James D. Watson, interviewed by John Rennie

In 1953 two young scientists, one American and the other British, announced that they had discovered the structure of DNA, the molecule that makes up genes. With that, the mystery of how parents' characteristics pass to offspring came to an end. Six years later, James D. Watson and Francis Crick received the Nobel Prize in medicine for their research, which has since been hailed as one of the most important scientific discoveries of the twentieth century. The "double helix" structure—which can be visualized as a pair of intertwined spiral staircases—became not just the symbol of DNA but a metaphor representing an individual's fundamental nature.

As part of a fiftieth anniversary celebration of the pair's historic accomplishment, *Scientific American*'s editor in chief, John Rennie, interviewed Watson about the discovery. In the following selection taken from that interview, Watson reports that a natural curiosity drove him to discover the structure of DNA so that he would have an explanation for life. He observes that the study of genetics is rapidly progressing and anticipates that the field may be played out in ten years. The next big area of research, Watson predicts, will be the study of how the brain functions. Brushing off popular fears about cloning and designer children, Watson asserts that the medical advances made possible by the discovery of DNA such as gene therapy will be positive contributions to humanity. After winning the Nobel Prize in 1962, Watson became director and later president of Cold Spring Harbor Laboratory on Long Island, New York.

Scientific American: *DNA is no longer just a scientific entity. It's erupted as this huge cultural phenomenon, as a metaphor for our natures. It's in our daily conversation, in art.*

When you were working on the double helix [structure of DNA], did you foresee DNA ever becoming this well known?

James Watson: No, no, we couldn't. Because no one had ever sequenced DNA or amplified DNA. It turned out to be totally wrong, but the famous Australian immunologist [Frank Macfarlene] Burnet published this article in a medical journal that came out in 1961 or 1962, in which he said DNA and molecular biology will not have an influence on medicine. Because [influence is] only possible when you can read the DNA. That's why the Human Genome Project is so important.

Neither [Francis] Crick nor I is very science-fiction oriented. We've always been more concerned with what exists. The value of predictions falls off radically after five years. Back in 1953, all we wanted to do was find out how DNA provided the information and what the cellular machinery was for making proteins. That's really all; we didn't think about gene therapy. It took about 15 years before people began to think about that, around 1968—once restriction enzymes came along and, soon after, DNA sequencing.

You've said that you first became involved with research on DNA because of your interests in evolution and information.

[Physicist Erwin] Schrödinger probably wasn't the first, but he was the first one I'd read to say that there must be a code of some kind that allowed molecules in cells to carry information. And in his book [*What Is Life?* (1944)], he doesn't even say "including information for proteins." It was that idea that there was a molecule in there which carried the information.

By the time Schrödinger's book came out, a few people like [biologist J.B.S.] Haldane were making that connection between genes and proteins. Back in those days the amino acid sequence for a protein hadn't been worked out. You knew there was some sequence, but that's all. It was only our getting the DNA structure and [chemist Frederick] Sanger sequencing the first polypeptide [protein] chain that let some air in.

An Inborn Curiosity

So would you say that your work was driven more by fascination with that idea than by ambition?

I was born curious. I would rather read economic history than history, for example, because I liked explanations. And so if you wanted an explanation for life, it had to be about the molecular basis for life. I never thought there was a spiritual basis for life; I was very lucky to be brought up by a father who had no religious beliefs. I didn't have that hang-up. My mother was nominally a Catholic, but that's as far as it went.

Looking back on the race for the double helix, it's obvious that individual personalities strongly influenced the specifics of who found it first and how. And yet the discovery at roughly that time also seems to have been inevitable. There were so many of you who were so close—you and Crick, Linus Pauling of the California Institute of Technology, Maurice Wilkins and Rosalind Franklin at King's College. If you and Crick had not made the discovery when you did—

I can't believe a year would have passed. We didn't know that Rosalind Franklin had in late February turned in the B form because she was leaving King's College. We didn't know her then. I still didn't know about it when I wrote *The Double Helix* (1968).

There has always been the controversy about Maurice Wilkins having shown you Rosalind Franklin's crystallography images without her permission, and that having given you and Francis an important clue to DNA's structure.

People have said, why didn't you talk to Rosalind later and thank her for seeing the picture? She didn't want to talk about it. She didn't talk to coworkers about it.

When she was dying, she stayed with Francis, and that might have been an occasion to reminisce about the past, but she was just "on with the future." She'd missed that one; she wanted to get the next one.

In retrospect, would it have been more appropriate for the Nobel to have been given to her, along with you and Francis, rather than to Maurice Wilkins?

The Prize Not Given

I think not. Wilkins gave us the crystalline photograph of the A form and she gave us the B form. So you could have said that in an ideal, perfect society, they would have gotten the chemistry prize and Crick and I would have gotten the biology prize. That would have been a nice way to honor the four of us. But no one thought that way.

We're very famous because DNA is very famous. If Rosalind had talked to Francis starting in 1951, shared her data with him, she would have solved that structure. And then she would have been the famous one.

On that Saturday morning [February 28, 1953, when Watson and Crick conceived of the double helix][1] we were proposing a model which we weren't sure was right. We had thought that x-ray data would then just be very decisive in making people believe it. Because [the model had suggested] a copying scheme that all the biologists wanted to believe in independently of the x-ray data.

Because the "A-T G-C" complementarity of the nucleotide bases would allow the double helix structure to make copies of itself.

We had thought we were going to get only half the way, you know? A proposal of the structure, and then somebody would prove the structure, and then you might have to ask how it was copied.

And instead it all came together at once. In a century we went from the point of rediscovering Mendel's laws and identifying chromosomes as agents of heredity to having the human genome largely worked out. Finding the double helix drops neatly in the middle of that span. How much, with respect to DNA, is left for us to do? Are there still major discoveries to be made, or is it all just filling in details?

The major problem, I think, is chromatin [the dynamic complex of DNA and histone proteins that makes up chromosomes]. What determines whether a given piece of DNA along the chromosome is functioning, since it's covered with the histones? What is happening at the level of methylation and epigenetics [chemical modification of the DNA that affects gene expression]? You can inherit something beyond the DNA sequence. That's where the real excitement of genetics is now.

And it seems to be moving pretty fast. You don't really want to make a guess, but I'd guess that over these next 10 years, the field will be pretty played out. A lot of very good people are working on it. We have the tools. At some stage, the basic principles of genetics will be known in terms of gene functioning, and then we'll be able to apply that more to problems like how the brain works.

RNA has also been moving out of DNA's shadow. We're now aware of phenomena like RNA interference, in which RNA molecules can counteract genes. Do we have the complexities of RNA

1. They announced their discovery on April 25, 1953.

dynamics still to crack? Is that comparable to the histone problem?

Yes, it's a lot more complex than we though in 1953. We thought there was just one form of RNA. But to make the RNA, you have to modify the histones. I think it's all the same—it's in the chromatin.

In a recent issue of *Nature*, Walter Gilbert of Harvard University wrote that "molecular biology is dead," largely because its subject, DNA, had been subsumed into every other field.

I agree with him, in the sense that it's a tool. Everything comes from DNA. So you can say you're studying DNA in canary behavior, or you can say you're studying canary behavior. I think we're studying canary behavior!

There are still very major problems to solve on how information is stored and retrieved and used in the brain. It's a bigger problem than DNA, and a more difficult one.

If you were starting out as a researcher now—

I'd be working on something about connections between genes and behavior. You can find genes for behaviors, but that doesn't tell you how the brain works. My first scientific interest was in how birds migrated. Until you know how the bird brain works, you're not going to know how genes can tell that bird where to migrate. Because, you know, that mother bird isn't telling the young one where to go! So it's got to be inherited.

There are lots of other big behavioral things [to solve]. Some people say they're mystified that men can like men, but I say, "It's just as mysterious as why men like women!"

These things are so difficult. Francis insists that brain research doesn't have [the equivalent of] a DNA molecule. It doesn't have a central thing from which everything else flows.

Do you have any opinion about how likely it is that someone will find something like that soon?

No. The young kids that go into it all hope that it will be while they're still young. And then they're likely to be part of that. So you try to pick a problem where you will be part of an enlightenment, but not the great enlightenment.

You have reputation for being outspoken, and get criticized for it. Do you have any regrets about things you've said?

Occasionally. Sometimes I've said things and later people have said, "Did you really need to say that?" because it seemed cruel. And sure, I've done that. But when no one is saying that we're going nowhere, someone has to. My loyalty has always been to make institutions as good as they could be.

I think there's something in me of that same weakness that is so apparent in [tennis champion] John McEnroe. I just can't sit while people are saying nonsense in a meeting without saying it's nonsense!

DNA's Other Discoverer

For half a century, you and Francis Crick have been bound together by history and the public imagination. Yet you don't really collaborate now and haven't for decades. How has your relationship changed? Are you still friends?

Yes, I think we are. He's almost like an older brother, with the 12-years difference between us. We tend to exchange information very fast, that is, we think the same way. Both of us are intellectually opposed to the idea that the truth comes from [divine] revelation. Francis has no interest in politics, and I don't know that he ever has. So in that sense, Francis thinks about science more than I do. Whereas I could easily get diverted.

On the subject of politics, many gene-related issues are in the public arena these days: genetically engineered foods, cloning, DNA fingerprinting and so on. How much confidence do you have in the political supervision of these?

I think they're so contentious that the state shouldn't enter in. Yes, I would just stay out of it, the way it should stay out of abortion. Reproductive decisions should be made by women, not the state.

I mean, cloning now is the issue. But the first clone is not like the first nuclear bomb going off. It's not going to hurt anyone!

If your health were lousy and your wife's health were lousy, and [the genetic illness] were in both your families, maybe you'd like to have a child who was healthy. I know a famous French scientist who never had children because there was madness in his family. He didn't want to take a chance on more madness. That's what I mean. Cloning might mean you would know there wasn't going to be any more madness. I think the paramount concern should be the rights of the family, as opposed to the rights of the state.

People say, "Well, these would be designer babies," and I say, "Well, what's wrong with designer clothes?" If you could just say, "My baby's not going to have asthma," wouldn't that be nice? What's wrong with therapeutic cloning? Who's being hurt?

Mystery of the Spirit

There's a mysticism about life. It's very understandable, if you're not a scientist, that you just can't quite see how it could all be molecules, and how you could start with this and end up with human consciousness and our complexity. Since we still don't know how the brain works, people say that we don't have it right. All we can say is, we don't think there's any spirit in a bacterium.

I remember when [physicist] Dick Feynman and I got identical letters back in 1964 from a California rabbi asking about our spiritual beliefs. I think Dick just wrote back that he had none. I was more polite because I wasn't Jewish [and didn't want to offend the rabbi], but I think that Dick could say what he thought. The problem in the United States is, it's not socially acceptable to be against god. Can religion ever be bad? That's not to be discussed. But in Europe it can be.

Does the public know enough about genetics to make these decisions prudently? Do you worry about people's abilities to debate the merits of genetically modified foods and the rest?

If you thought every plant was the product of a god who put it there for a purpose, you could say that you shouldn't change it. But America isn't what it was like when the Pilgrims came here. We've changed everything. We've never tried to respect the past, we've tried to improve on it. And I think any desire to stop people from improving things would be against the human spirit.

An Introduction to Gene Therapy

By David Petechuk

Gene therapy, as David Petechuk explains in the following selection, has emerged from the study of heredity to become one of the hottest fields in medical research. At its core lies the principle that genetically caused conditions can be cured by the insertion of corrective genes. There are two basic approaches to making such a correction, Petechuk explains: somatic therapy, in which genes are inserted into the tissues of a living person, and germ-line therapy, in which genes are introduced into sperm or eggs to become part of the inheritable genome. In either case, he says, some vehicle is required to transport the replacement genes into the target cells. Scientists have relied largely on viruses to do the transporting, but, as Petechuk relates, viruses raise safety concerns. For example, if the patient sneezes, the virus could infect others nearby. In consequence, scientists have been experimenting with other means of delivering genes, such as shooting tiny gold pellets laden with corrective genes into the patient's body.

Since its inception, Petechuk says, gene therapy has come to be seen as a promising avenue for cures not only for entirely genetic conditions such as hemophilia but also for many other ailments, including cancer, where genes play some role in determining susceptibility. David Petechuk writes on scientific topics.

Gene therapy is a rapidly growing field of medicine in which genes are introduced into the body to treat diseases. Genes control heredity and provide the basic biological code for determining a cell's specific functions. Gene therapy seeks to provide genes that correct or supplant the disease-controlling functions of cells that are not, in essence, doing their job. Somatic gene therapy introduces therapeutic genes at the tissue or cellular level to treat a specific individual. Germ-line gene therapy inserts genes into reproductive cells or into embryos to correct genetic defects that could be passed on to future generations. Initially conceived as an approach for treating inherited diseases, like cystic fibrosis and Huntington's disease, the scope of potential gene therapies has grown to include treatments for cancers, arthritis, and infectious diseases. Although gene therapy testing in humans has advanced rapidly, many questions surround its use. For example, some scientists are concerned that the therapeutic genes themselves may cause disease. Others fear that germ-line gene therapy may be used to control human development in ways not connected with disease, like intelligence or appearance.

Gene therapy has grown out of the science of genetics or how heredity works. Scientists know that life begins in a cell, the basic building block of all multicellular organisms. Humans, for instance, are made up of trillions of cells, each performing a specific function. Within the cell's nucleus (the center part of a cell that regulates its chemical functions) are pairs of chromosomes. These threadlike structures are made up of a single molecule of DNA (deoxyribonucleic acid), which carries the blueprint of life in the form of codes, or genes, that determine inherited characteristics.

A DNA molecule looks like two ladders with one of the sides taken off both and then twisted around each other. The rungs of these ladders meet (resulting in a spiral staircase–like structure) and are called base pairs. Base pairs are made up of nitrogen molecules and arranged in specific sequences. Millions of these base pairs, or sequences, can make up a single gene, specifically defined as a segment of the chromosome and DNA that contains certain hereditary information. The gene, or combination of genes formed by these base pairs ultimately direct an organism's growth and characteristics through the production of certain chemicals, primarily proteins, which carry out most of the body's chemical functions and biological reactions.

Scientists have long known that defects in genes present within cells can cause inherited diseases like cystic fibrosis, sickle-cell anemia, and hemophilia. Similarly, errors in entire chromosomes can cause disease, like Down Syndrome or Turner's Syndrome. As the study of genetics advanced, however, scientists learned that an altered genetic sequence can also make people more susceptible to diseases that are not necessarily inherited, like atherosclerosis, cancer, and even schizophrenia. These diseases have a genetic component, but are also influenced by environmental factors (like diet and lifestyle). The objective of gene therapy is to treat diseases by introducing functional genes into the body to alter the cells involved in the disease process by either replacing missing genes or providing copies of functioning genes to replace defective ones. The inserted genes can be naturally-occurring genes that produce the desired effect or may be genetically engineered (or altered) genes.

Scientists have known how to manipulate a gene's structure in the laboratory since the early 1970s through a process called gene splicing. The process involves removing a fragment of DNA containing the specific genetic sequence desired, then inserting it into the DNA of another gene. The resultant product is called recombinant DNA and the process is genetic engineering.

Two Kinds of Therapy

There are basically two types of gene therapy. Germ-line gene therapy introduces genes into reproductive cells (sperm and eggs) or into embryos in hopes of correcting genetic defects that could be passed on to future generations. Most of the current work in applying gene therapy, however, has been in the realm of somatic gene therapy. In this type of gene therapy, therapeutic genes are inserted into tissue or cells to produce a naturally occurring protein or substance that is lacking or not functioning correctly in an individual patient.

In both types of therapy, scientists need something to transport either the entire gene or a recombinant DNA to the cell's nucleus, where the chromosomes and DNA reside. In essence, vectors are molecular delivery trucks. One of the first and most popular vectors developed was viruses because they invade cells as part of the natural infection process. Viruses have the potential to be excellent vectors because they have a specific relationship with the host in that they colonize certain cell types and tissues in specific organs. As a result, vectors are chosen according to their affinity for certain cells and areas of the body.

One of the first vectors used was retroviruses. Because these viruses are easily cloned (artificially reproduced) in the laboratory, scientists have studied them extensively and learned a great deal about their biological action. They have also learned how to remove the genetic information which governs viral replication, thus reducing the chances of infection.

Retroviruses work best in actively dividing cells, but cells in the body are relatively stable and do not divide often. As a result, these cells are used primarily for ex vivo (outside the body) manipulation. First, the cells are removed from the patient's body, and the virus, or vector, carrying the gene is inserted into them. Next, the cells are placed into a nutrient culture where they grow and replicate. Once enough cells are gathered, they are returned to the body, usually by injection into the blood stream. Theoretically, as long as these cells survive, they will provide the desired therapy.

Another class of viruses, called the adenoviruses, may also prove to be good gene vectors. These cells can effectively infect nondividing cells in the body, where the desired gene product is then expressed naturally. In addition to being a more efficient approach to gene transportation, these viruses, which cause respiratory infections, are more easily purified and made stable than retroviruses, resulting in less chance of an unwanted viral infection. However, these viruses live for several days in the body, and some concern surrounds the possibility of infecting others with the viruses through sneezing or coughing. Other viral vectors include influenza viruses, Sindbis virus, and a herpes virus that infects nerve cells.

Working Without Viruses

Scientists have also delved into nonviral vectors. These vectors rely on the natural biological process in which cells uptake (or gather) macromolecules. One approach is to use liposomes, globules of fat produced by the body and taken up by cells. Scientists are also investigating the introduction of raw recombinant DNA by injecting it into the bloodstream or placing it on microscopic beads of gold shot into the skin with a "genegun." Another possible vector under development is based on dendrimer molecules. A class of polymers (naturally occurring or artificial substances that have a high molecular weight and formed by smaller molecules of the same or similar substances), is "constructed" in the laboratory by combining these smaller molecules. They have been used in manufacturing Styrofoam, polyethylene cartons, and Plexiglass. In the laboratory, dendrimers have shown the ability to transport genetic material into human cells. They can also be designed to form an affinity for particular cell membranes by attaching to certain sugars and protein groups. . . .

Many Targets for Gene Therapy

The potential scope of gene therapy is enormous. More than 4,200 diseases have been identified as resulting directly from defective genes, and countless others that may be partially influenced by a person's genetic makeup. Initial research has concentrated on developing gene therapies for diseases whose genetic origins have been established and for other diseases that can be cured or ameliorated by substances genes produce.

The following are examples of potential gene therapies. People suffering from cystic fibrosis lack a gene needed to produce a salt-regulating protein. This protein regulates the flow of chloride into epithelial cells, which cover the air passages of the nose and lungs. Without this regulation, cystic fibrosis patients suffer from a buildup of a thick mucus, which can cause lung infections and respiratory problems, which usually lead to death within the first 29 years of life. A gene therapy technique to correct this defect might employ an adenovirus to transfer a normal copy of what scientists call the cystic fibrosis transmembrane conductance regulator, or CTRF, gene. The gene is introduced into the patient by spraying it into the nose or lungs.

Familial hypercholesterolemia (FH) is also an inherited disease, resulting in the inability to process cholesterol properly, which leads to high levels of artery-clogging fat in the blood stream. FH patients often suffer heart attacks and strokes because of blocked arteries. A gene therapy approach used to battle FH is much more intricate than most gene therapies because it involves partial surgical removal of patients' livers (ex vivo transgene therapy). Corrected copies of a gene that serve to reduce cholesterol build-up are inserted into the liver sections, which are then transplanted back into the patients.

Gene therapy has also been tested on AIDS patients. AIDS is caused by the human immunodeficiency virus (HIV), which weakens the body's immune system to the point that sufferers are unable to fight off diseases like killer pneumonias and cancer. In one approach, genes that produce specific HIV proteins have been altered to stimulate immune system functioning without causing the negative effects that a complete HIV molecule has on the immune system. These genes are then injected in the patient's blood stream. Another approach to treating AIDS is to insert, via white blood cells, genes that have been genetically engineered to produce a receptor that would attract HIV and reduce its chances of replicating.

Taking On Cancer

Several cancers also have the potential to be treated with gene therapy. A therapy tested for melanoma, or skin cancer, involves introducing a gene with an anticancer protein called tumor necrosis factor (TNF) into test tube samples of the patient's own cancer cells, which are then reintroduced into the patient. In brain cancer, the approach is to insert a specific gene that increases the cancer cells' susceptibility to a common drug used in fighting the disease.

Gaucher's disease is an inherited disease caused by a mutant gene that inhibits the production of an enzyme called glucocerebrosidase. Gaucher patients have enlarged livers and spleens and eventually their bones fall apart. Clinical gene therapy trials focus on inserting the gene for producing this enzyme.

Gene therapy is also being considered as an approach to solving a problem associated with a surgical procedure known as balloon angioplasty. In this procedure, a stent (in this case, a type of tubular scaffolding) is used to open the clogged artery. However, in response to the trauma of the stent insertion, the body initiates a natural healing process that produces too many cells in the artery and results in restenosis, or reclosing of the artery. The gene therapy approach to preventing this unwanted side effect is to cover the outside of the stents with a soluble gel. This gel contains vectors for genes that would reduce this overactive healing response. . . .

The Future of Gene Therapy

Gene therapy seems elegantly simple in its concept: supply the human body with a gene that can correct a biological malfunction that causes a disease. However, there are many obstacles and some distinct questions concerning the viability of gene therapy. For example, viral vectors must be carefully controlled lest they infect the patient with a viral disease. Some vectors, like retroviruses, can also enter cells functioning properly and interfere with the natural biological processes, possibly leading to other diseases. Other viral vectors, like the adenoviruses, are often recognized and destroyed by the immune system so their therapeutic effects are short-lived. Maintaining gene expression so it performs its role

properly after vector delivery is difficult. As a result, some therapies need to be repeated often to provide long-lasting benefits.

One of the most pressing issues, however, is gene regulation.
Genes work in concert to regulate their functioning. In other
words, several genes may play a part in turning other genes on and
off. For example, certain genes work together to stimulate cell division and growth, but if these are not regulated, the inserted genes
could cause tumor formation and cancer. Another difficulty is
learning how to make the gene go into action only when needed.
For the best and safest therapeutic effort, a specific gene should
turn on, for example, when certain levels of a protein or enzyme
are low and must be replaced. But the gene should also remain
dormant when not needed to ensure it doesn't oversupply a substance and disturb the body's delicate chemical makeup.

One approach to gene regulation is to attach other genes that
detect certain biological activities and then react as a type of au-
tomatic off-and-on switch that regulates the activity of the other
genes according to biological cues. Although still in the rudimentary stages, researchers are making headway in inhibiting some
gene functioning by using a synthetic DNA to block gene tran-
scriptions (the copying of genetic information). This approach
may have implications for gene therapy.

Thorny Ethical Issues

While gene therapy holds promise as a revolutionary approach to
treating disease, ethical concerns over its use and ramifications
have been expressed by scientists and laypeople alike. For example, since much needs to be learned about how these genes actually work and their long-term effect, is it ethical to test these therapies on humans, where they could have a disastrous result? As
with most clinical trials concerning new therapies, including many
drugs, the patients participating in these studies have usually not
responded to more established therapies and are often so ill the
novel therapy is their only hope for long-term survival.

Another questionable outgrowth of gene therapy is that scientists could possibly manipulate genes to genetically control traits
in human offspring that are not health related. For example, perhaps a gene could be inserted to ensure that a child would not be
bald, a seemingly harmless goal. However, what if genetic manipulation was used to alter skin color, prevent homosexuality, or

ensure good looks? If a gene is found that can enhance intelligence of children who are not yet born, will everyone in society, the rich and the poor, have access to the technology or will it be so expensive only the elite can afford it?

The Human Genome Project, which plays such an integral role for the future of gene therapy, also has social repercussions. If individual genetic codes can be determined, will such information be used against people? For example, will someone more susceptible to a disease have to pay higher insurance premiums or be denied health insurance altogether? Will employers discriminate between two potential employees, one with a "healthy" genome and the other with genetic defects?

Echoes of the Eugenics Abuses

Some of these concerns can be traced back to the eugenics movement popular in the first half of the 20th century. This genetic "philosophy" was a societal movement that encouraged people with "positive" traits to reproduce while those with less desirable traits were sanctioned from having children. Eugenics was used to pass strict immigration laws in the United States, barring less suitable people from entering the country lest they reduce the quality of the country's collective gene pool. Probably the most notorious example of eugenics in action was the rise of Nazism in Germany, which resulted in the Eugenic Sterilization Law of 1933. The law required sterilization for those suffering from certain disabilities and even for some who were simply deemed "ugly." To ensure that this novel science is not abused, many governments have established organizations specifically for overseeing the development of gene therapy. In the United States, the Food and Drug Administration and the National Institutes of Health requires scientists to take a precise series of steps and meet stringent requirements before approving clinical trials.

In fact, gene therapy has been immersed in more controversy and surrounded by more scrutiny in both the health and ethical arena than most other technologies (except, perhaps, for cloning) that promise to substantially change society. Despite the health and ethical questions surrounding gene therapy, the field will continue to grow and is likely to revolutionize medicine faster than any previous medical advancement.

CHAPTER 2

The Road
to Success

The First Human Gene Therapy Trial

By Jeff Lyon and Peter Gorner

Subjects who volunteer for research trials often do so knowing that they stand little chance of personal benefit. Yet their bravery can be of immense value to others. In the selection that follows, taken from their book *Altered Fates: Gene Therapy and the Retooling of Human Life*, Jeff Lyon and Peter Gorner describe the first human gene therapy trial, in which Maurice Kuntz, a terminally ill cancer patient, took part. They explain that in 1989 surgeon W. French Anderson attempted to save Kuntz's life by injecting specially modified tumor-infiltrating lymphocytes, or TILs, into his body. TILs ordinarily move through the corridors of the body's lymphatic system and home in on bacteria and other threats, and destroy them. TILs have only a modest ability to suppress tumors, so scientists on Anderson's team sought to turn extracted TILs into better-targeted warriors by splicing in genes that would help researchers to track and guide them toward tumors. After successfully splicing, Anderson and his team reinserted the TILs into Kuntz' body.

According to Lyon and Gorner, at first the technique appeared to be working—Kuntz showed no ill effects from the treatment and the number of cancer cells in his body decreased. However, within months the cancer had spread to his brain. Kuntz died on Easter Sunday, 1990. Lyon and Gorner report that despite Kuntz's death, this first human experiment involving rudimentary gene therapy was hailed as a significant medical advance. Lyon and Gorner, reporters for the *Chicago Tribune*, won the 1987 Pulitzer Prize for explanatory journalism.

On March 13, 1989, Maurice and Sharon Kuntz made their first trip to Bethesda [Maryland]. "We'd never heard of NIH [National Institutes of Health]," Sharon admits. "We initially paid our own way, but after Maurice was accepted, they paid for everything, even the motel. They were very nice. Very caring." The couple's spirits rose after tests revealed that Maurice was the perfect candidate for TIL [tumor-infiltrating lymphocyte] therapy. A brain scan, in particular, was very important: it showed no cancer there, which was crucial because TIL therapy is unable to cross the blood-brain barrier and do battle against brain tumors.

"They explained about TILs to us in a simplified way," Sharon says. "There was no pressure. They even said Maurice could die from the therapy. But we made friends. They weren't just other people in the waiting room. All the TIL candidates would go back at the same time. It became a family. There was a bond. When we walked into the clinical center, it was like a weight was lifted from our shoulders. Maurice had people with him twenty-four hours a day. He had the best care anyone could have ever wanted." What the Kuntzes didn't know was that, as a candidate for TIL therapy and gene transfer, Maurice Kuntz was viewed by NIH professionals as having no more than three months to live.

Black Tumor

On March 20, in a ninety-minute operation, government surgeons removed a cancerous tumor directly above Kuntz's right breastbone. "They told me they couldn't guarantee they got everything," says Sharon, "but they got everything they could see. The tumor was black, like the mole. It was melanoma."

As Kuntz began to recover from his surgery, he had not yet met [gene therapy pioneer and surgeon] French Anderson. But Anderson already knew him intimately. [Dr. Steven] Rosenberg's new comrade-in-arms, working in his cramped laboratory, a lump forming in his throat at the thought of the milestone soon to come, had begun extracting TILs' from Kuntz's tumor, which was about the size of a small plum. When he mixed about 50 million tumor cells with IL-2 [interleukin-2], they all died, being replaced by a rich crop of multiplying TILs, which had been hiding out in the tumor. Not only did IL-2 boost the TILs' numbers exponentially; it strengthened their anticancer tendencies until they were acting like frenzied ninjas. Normally, this would take about a month, but

Maurice Kuntz's TILs seemed to be growing extraordinarily well. In the meantime, Kuntz, feeling better, was released on March 24. He flew home and went back to work on the twenty-eighth. In Bethesda, tending to his fast-growing cultures, a marveling French Anderson even started to seed separate batches of Maurice Kuntz's TILs, one without the marker gene and one that he hoped would be given the bacterial gene, by means of [medical researcher] Dusty Miller's retroviral vector. A month later, the couple were summoned back for the first round of ordinary TIL therapy. That was on April 26. "Nobody had said anything about the gene yet," Sharon recalls. Scheduled for his first treatment on the twenty-eighth, Maurice was visited the night before by Anderson. The white-haired scientist introduced himself and spent two hours with the couple, getting to know them. He put up his feet and relaxed, and with his customary Tulsa [Oklahoma] charm told them about [his wife] Kathy and their cocker spaniels.

Childless Doctor

The Andersons had decided to remain childless and pursue their careers, but over the years the couple has developed relationships with several "surrogate kids" from broken homes, treating them like family, assisting them through college and even medical school, shepherding their careers. Anderson bragged to the Kuntzes about them. He related that he had been fortunate enough to study in England and described where he worked at NIH. No hotshot gene surgeon then, he was as likable as a teddy bear.

"He was humble when he talked about his work," Sharon says. "I don't remember him mentioning the word 'gene,' but I really liked him. Maurice did, too." The next day, Kuntz received ordinary TIL therapy. The couple had been warned to expect severe side effects, but there were some other problems as well. During the first infusion of cells, doctors punctured Kuntz's lung while putting in an intravenous tube. A chest tube had to be inserted to help him breathe. . . .

By Saturday, May 13, Kuntz had recovered sufficiently to be sent home again. In discussing his options, the NIH doctors had told him about gene transfer. "Count me in, if you need me," Kuntz told them. Recalls Sharon, "They told us it had never been done before, but we didn't mind that. Maurice really didn't think it could help him, but he hoped it might eventually help somebody else. So he told them, sure, if they wanted him to go first, he would do it." Back home in Indiana, an urgent phone call from NIH interrupted Kuntz's rest: Steven Rosenberg and French Anderson wanted to talk to him about receiving gene-marked TIL cells in a second round of TIL therapy. Right away. The couple flew back to Bethesda on May 21 and was directly admitted to the intensive-care unit. "I left the kids home," Sharon says. "They stayed with friends—our closest friends knew what was going on. I didn't want the kids with us, in case something went wrong."

That night, Anderson again came to see them and spent three hours this time. More earnest now, he told the couple the details of the experiment, going over every point, expressing his hope that the marker gene would track the TILs to Kuntz's tumors like radio collars on wolves, so that Rosenberg could see where they went and what they were up to. Anderson reiterated to Kuntz that he didn't *have* to do it; that he didn't have to go first; that he might suffer a heart attack from the gene transfer, or even worse. Kuntz nodded. He understood. Anderson carefully read the couple every word of the informed consent. They signed it. Then Rosenberg came into the room beaming with his customary cheer. "We'd met him before," Sharon says, "but we didn't have the same relationship with him as with French. Maurice and French became good friends." At eleven-thirty that fateful night, May 21, 1989, Sharon left her husband to catch a cab back to her motel. Anderson, driving by, saw her waiting and insisted on taking her home.

A Long Shot

To Anderson, the gene transfer TIL experiment "was like a moonshot," pervaded by the nail-biting complexities, shattering last-minute delays, and harrowing suspense that NASA [National Aeronautics and Space Administration] had made a trademark. The team had received permission from federal regulators months before to treat a total of ten metastatic melanoma patients with gene-marked TILs. But the "final go," in Anderson's molecular moonshot had come only on May 20, 1989, after a complicated countdown that hinged on about twenty different factors—the delicate preparation of living cells had to be perfect, and the perfect patient candidate had to be in the perfect state of readiness to receive them. Previous countdowns had not made it that far. In fact, Maurice Kuntz was actually the third final candidate. Discouraging laboratory telemetry had spooked Anderson into abruptly canceling one molecular launch twenty-four hours before infusion, and another had been scrubbed with only ten minutes left.

But all systems were go on the morning of May 22, 1989. In the privacy of the surgical intensive-care ward of the 550-bed NIH clinical center, Anderson, Rosenberg, and [colleague Michael] Blaese hovered over the bedside of Maurice Kuntz, a patient identified in news accounts only as "a 52-year-old man dying of cancer." He was undergoing a massive transfusion, with the first of five plastic bags holding 200 billion of his own tumor-fighting white cells that had been culled from his biopsied cancer and

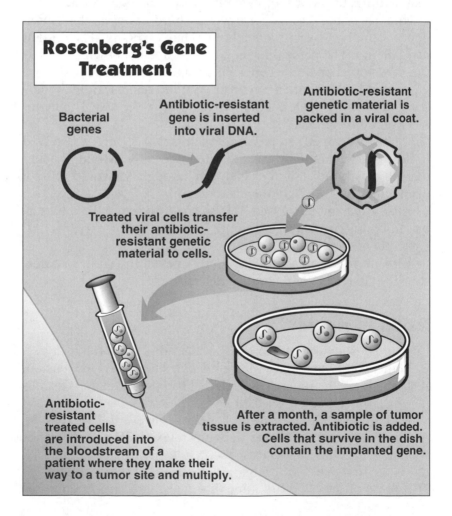

Rosenberg's Gene Treatment

Bacterial genes

Antibiotic-resistant gene is inserted into viral DNA.

Antibiotic-resistant genetic material is packed in a viral coat.

Treated viral cells transfer their antibiotic-resistant genetic material to cells.

Antibiotic-resistant treated cells are introduced into the bloodstream of a patient where they make their way to a tumor site and multiply.

After a month, a sample of tumor tissue is extracted. Antibiotic is added. Cells that survive in the dish contain the implanted gene.

supercharged in the lab. As Kuntz, wearing a white hospital gown with blue polka dots, sat propped up on a hospital bed, bristling monitors like a porcupine, holding hands with his wife through the side rails, a nurse hooked up a plastic intravenous bag containing the milky fluid. "Maurice was not nervous. He was very calm, but I had been praying all morning," Sharon remembers. "We were watching each other the whole time. Smiling at each other. Just looking at each other." Nobody said anything historic, she says. The atmosphere was too tense for that. A male nurse stood quietly in the background holding a syringe filled with adrenaline in case resuscitation was required. But without ado, the IV dripped into Kuntz as the seconds ticked by. And in this intimate setting, the course of medicine was changed forever. . . .

Nobody could say for sure what would happen when alien genes actually were introduced into a human being. They might just kill him. The persons around the bedside held their breath as the IV dripped and new genes entered the human bloodstream. "You could have heard a pin drop," Sharon relates. Both Anderson and Rosenberg checked their watches: 10:47 A.M. The molecular moon rocket had lifted off.

"Maurice seemed serene," Anderson recalls. "But I was scared to death. My worst fear was that the impossible would happen: that after everything all of us had been through, he would suffer a heart attack and die right then and there!"

Finally, one minute passed. "He's okay," Anderson thought, surprised by his own success. Kuntz just sat comfortably, a small smile playing at his lips.

Three minutes passed. "Absolutely uneventful," noted Anderson. The first stage of the rocket disengaged.

Relief in Humor

Five minutes. "Perfectly normal." The second stage fell away.

At this point, the patient himself decided to lighten the tension. Alluding to all the mouse research that had preceded this first human experiment, Kuntz cracked, "Well, I haven't grown a tail yet."

That broke the ice. Various jokes about cheese followed as the minutes stretched and the participants relaxed a little. The genes were now in orbit. Steven Rosenberg, as usual, was jubilant. "Today is the first ever!" he obligingly declared for the benefit of the NIH press office, "the first time that a new gene has been introduced into a human." Later that day, a new sign appeared on the wall of Anderson's office: "One small step for a gene, but a giant leap for genetics."

"French was like an excited kid who wanted to jump up and down," Sharon confides. Yet, as she recalls it today, the full import of the moment had not sunk in for her and her husband. "Even though we'd been told what a milestone it was, it wasn't such a great big thing to us. At the time we both were focusing on Maurice. He even later told other patients it was no big thing, just a tracer bullet. He didn't feel it was a foreign gene. He said he knew it wouldn't hurt him."

The first infusion lasted about forty-five minutes. As the cells dripped into a central line on the left side of Kuntz's body—the IV penetrated the subclavian vein that led straight to his heart—[Surgical Resident Susan] Calabro withdrew blood from another intravenous line in his right arm. Left side in, right side out. Input, output. First, the blood samples were to indicate how the TILs and their new genes immediately fared in their big survival test as they passed through the lungs, liver, and spleen—the giant filters that cleanse the labyrinthine tubing of the circulatory system. Together, these obstacles were tantamount to a black hole, so far as gene science was concerned. The cells could easily have vanished forever. . . .

A Perfect Performance

The TIL cells and their genes were designed to persist, or stay in orbit—for months, it was hoped—and Anderson and Rosenberg would monitor them periodically, depending on the availability of the patients and whether their tumors were capable of being biopsied. "But the early data represented the first time that TILs have ever been detected in the bloodstream," enthused Anderson a week after the first experiment. "Using radioactive tracers, they never were found. Not even immediately during infusion." If, by some incredible fluke, the delivery virus had somehow started to replicate in Kuntz's bloodstream, PCR [polymerase chain reaction, a DNA detection test] should have picked up that signal, too. "We asked the PCR to look for the presence of the virus's envelope gene," Anderson said. "It found none. So the virus has done precisely what it was designed to do. It performed perfectly. We couldn't be happier.". . .

At first, it looked as if the TILs would save Maurice Kuntz. "We drove [back] to Bethesda in June," Sharon notes. "Maurice felt good. He had no pain. Tests showed that some of the mets [metastases, or lesions] in his liver, and in his spleen, had disappeared. So he had hope. It looked like it was working." Kuntz fished the summer away, seemed to feel okay. He went back to Bethesda for more TIL therapy, without the bacterial gene, but the regimen seemed to have run its course. That November, Kuntz somehow found the strength to prune his spruce trees. "I want them to look pretty for you in the spring," he told Sharon. A chill seized her heart. "I think deep down he knew," she says. Three metastases had spread to his brain.

The Cancer Strikes Back

After that, things rolled downhill fast. In November, Rosenberg treated Kuntz's brain cancer with radiation and removed his spleen, which again had become cancerous. Anderson grew new TILs from it, and the team tried another bout of TIL therapy on Kuntz. It had worked in the past. At home, Sharon stood by while her husband received repeated radiation treatments—eleven in all—which dehydrated him and made him sicker and sicker. Finally, in desperation, Sharon called NIH and pleaded, "If he is going to die, please don't let him die this way." NIH flew the couple out immediately and pumped Kuntz full of fats and fluids—but no more TILs—so that he could spend Christmas home with his family.

More metastases kept developing. At this point, Anderson took Sharon aside and leveled with her: "Enjoy the time you have together," he gently advised. "How much time do we have?" she wanted to know. "Nobody knows but God," Anderson replied, "but maybe six to eight weeks."

Back home again, Kuntz took to his bed. He began telling Sharon what to do: keep the house, sell the van and buy a car, get the chimney cleaned, trim the pine trees. The family doctor made several house calls. "I want to keep him here," Sharon told him. "No more hospitals." The doctor told her she was doing as good a job as any hospital.

Up until the end, Maurice Kuntz was aware of everything around him. He refused morphine, yet seemed to be in no pain, his wife says. Friends and family came to call. Sharon nursed him through the nights. "We wanted him to know he was with people he loved," she says. "He told me, 'I'm ready to go to see Mom now.'"

Death with Dignity

Finally, at 6 A.M. on Easter Sunday 1990, nearly a year after he made medical history, Maurice Kuntz quietly died after a long and valiant fight. That night, his body was flown to NIH for autopsy and then home for burial. French Anderson, who had been on vacation with his wife in Hawaii, had tried to get home for the autopsy, but to no avail. "But they did it as carefully and with dignity as if it were surgery," he reassured Sharon. "They did it as if he were going to wake up."

"And I know they did," Sharon softly says, her own love and respect filling her voice. "I feel my husband was chosen to have cancer. He told me, 'I'm glad it's me, instead of one of my brothers.' That was the kind of man he was.

"I only wish he could have known that because of him gene therapy was so soon to come to pass. He would have been so proud to have helped a small child."

The First Genuine Success

**By W. French Anderson,
interviewed by Kathleen McAuliffe**

In 1989 W. French Anderson turned his attention to curing genetic disease in children. The Harvard-trained physician had long wanted to apply gene therapy to such cures, according to this selection from an interview he gave to the science magazine *Omni*. The breakthrough came with a four-year-old girl named Ashanti DeSilva, who was suffering from a disease now known as severe combined immunodeficiency, or SCID for short. (In the selection it is referred to as ADA, for the missing enzyme.) The disease, which robs a person of the ability to overcome infection, first made a popular impression in the 1980s with the case of David Demaret, who became known as the "Bubble Boy" because he lived until his premature death inside a plastic shield meant to protect him from contact with any germs.

As Anderson explains, to save DeSilva's life, he removed white blood cells from the young patient, infused them with viruses bearing corrective genes, and then reinserted them into her body. After repeated treatments, she began to display normal immune functions. At the time of the interview, the long-term success of the treatment was uncertain, but as of 2003 DeSilva remains healthy, although her body still requires booster shots of the enzyme she was born lacking. As a result of this success, Anderson became known as the "father of gene therapy." He continues his stellar career as director of the gene therapy laboratories at the University of Southern California. However, gene therapy for SCID has since been suspended because some other patients have come down with a form of cancer apparently resulting from the treatment—a possibility that Anderson himself acknowledged in the interview with *Omni* editor Kathleen McAuliffe that follows.

Kathleen McAuliffe, "W. French Anderson," *Omni*, vol. 13, July 1991, p. 62. Copyright © 1991 by Omni Publications International, Ltd. Reproduced by permission.

H e always knew what he wanted to do. In the late Fifties, before recombinant DNA technology was drawing-board theory, he vowed to cure hereditary disorders by repairing faulty genes. His Harvard professors laughed at the aspiring genetic surgeon with the Okie accent and cowboy boots. But W. French Anderson, now chief of the Molecular Hematology Branch at the National Heart, Lung, Blood Institute in Bethesda, Maryland, never wavered in his mission to bring gene therapy from the laboratory bench to the patient's bedside. And in September 1990, Anderson and his colleagues ushered in a new era of medicine with the first human gene procedure aimed at correcting a hereditary disease.

The patient, a four-year-old girl, was born with an adenosine deaminase (ADA) deficiency. She lacked the same key immune cell enzyme as David the bubble boy, whose defenses were so impaired that he was forced to live inside a germ-free capsule. Anderson and collaborators R. Michael Blaese and Kenneth Culver of the National Cancer Institute (NCI) combined some of the girl's white blood cells with those of an engineered virus. These genetically modified cells were then reintroduced into her bloodstream, where it was hoped they would multiply over the coming months, gradually restoring the functioning of her immune system.

Although still too soon to predict the ultimate success of this much-heralded trial, the physicians are very encouraged by the child's progress. She is better clinically and many of her immune function studies are improving, some into the normal range. Another ADA patient, a nine-year-old girl, began treatment on January 31, 1991. Early results suggest that she, too, is improving thanks to gene therapy. The investigators now believe this general strategy promises to have applications far beyond the treatment of rare hereditary diseases. Since genes code for vital body chemicals, Anderson thinks gene transfer techniques will eventually be used to "trick" cells into releasing drugs useful in the treatment of almost any disorder—from AIDS and cancer to heart disease and ordinary aging. Inserting the gene for insulin into the B cells of the pancreas might enable the diabetic patient to synthesize his own internal source of the hormone, eliminating the need for daily injections.

Raised at the edge of the dust bowl in Tulsa, Anderson was a prodigy. His passion for science burgeoned at age three, and by the end of grade school, he'd consumed every technical book he could find, including college-level medical texts. As a Harvard University senior at seventeen, he took one of the first courses linking DNA to genetics. The instructor was James Watson, the Nobel laureate who only four years earlier had codiscovered the chemical structure of DNA with Francis Crick. A year later, Anderson went to Cambridge, England, to continue his genetic studies with Crick. He completed his M.D. at Harvard in 1963 and two years later moved to the National Institutes of Health, where he's been ever since. . . .

Kathleen McAuliffe first interviewed Anderson in his office, and later in the more relaxed environment of his home. Well . . . relaxed for French Anderson. Afterward, he went to his cellar gym to practice karate, demonstrating once again his iron will—and iron fist.

Omni: Tampering with genes—even for treating diseases—has aroused widespread concerns. Do you think those fears are inflated?

Anderson: It's clearly an emotional issue. Jeremy Rifkin [outspoken critic of genetic engineering] has fanned those concerns by exaggerating the risks. But he wouldn't attract so much media attention if society didn't have fears in the first place. Yes, I am concerned. My mother is concerned. The athletes I accompanied to the Olympics are concerned. It's bad enough to have your mind manipulated through advertising, or into eating artificial substances in foods. So the notion of manipulating genes—which make us who we are—is frightening. I feel strongly that gene therapy should be applied only for the treatment of disease. Very firm lines should be drawn to ensure that genetic engineering is used for no other purpose. That's been my position for twenty-five years.

I believe an excellent system is in place for reviewing protocols and that doctors in this area are following a very ethical path. The long, involved process of gaining approval for the first human gene therapy trial is testimony to the numerous safeguards in place. This [he points to a document bigger than a Manhattan phone book] was the earliest draft of the protocol for the experiment. The Recombinant DNA Advisory Committee and half a dozen other regulatory committees studied it. Several reviewed the experiment twice, and numerous public hearings took place with TV crews present. In the end, virtually every reviewer voted to proceed with the experiment. Even Rifkin complimented us on the care we took in preparing the Informed Consent Document that lays out for the patient all the risks and benefits of the procedure.

Why did you choose a patient with ADA deficiency, a very rare disorder, for the first gene therapy trial?

In the Seventies I initially targeted a more common hereditary disorder—thalassemia—for the first trial. Kids with the disease produce abnormal hemoglobin [the blood molecule that transports oxygen]. Those pictures on the wall are of Nick and Judy, my first two patients with thalassemia. It's a fatal disease, and both died years ago. Unfortunately, thalassemia turned out to be too great a challenge for us then because the instructions for producing hemoglobin are encoded in several different genes.

Isn't it distressing talking to these desperately ill children?

I'm much more comfortable with children than adults, who tend to maintain a protective front. Kids talk about things important to them. Death and suffering are very real issues. Yes, I'm very comfortable talking to them about dying, I interact well with sick children. I can just feel with them.

Why was ADA deficiency a better disease to target than thalassemia?

ADA, which stands for the enzyme that malfunctions in these children as a result of their genetic defect, involves only one gene. Without adenosine deaminase, the body cannot produce new T and B lymphocytes. So ADA kids suffer from severe combined immunodeficiency and need to be protected from infections.

How is gene therapy done?

We withdraw the children's white blood cells and put into each cell a healthy copy of the gene for the ADA enzyme. We'd already genetically modified monkeys' immune cells, and after we reintroduced the white blood cells intravenously, the animals actually produced human ADA in their bloodstreams. That positive result convinced us we were ready to begin treating a human with the disease.

Could you be guilty of rushing ahead too quickly, as critics claim?

Some patients with ADA might have been helped had we proceeded three years earlier. Richard Mulligan [at the Whitehead Institute for Biomedical Research in Boston] is the main scientist opposing our group. And from his perspective, he is right. But as a Ph.D., he doesn't have the experience of an M.D. doing rounds on a pediatric ward every day who knows that ninety percent of medicine is an art—not a science. That makes a scientist uncomfortable. So he felt our ADA gene protocol was premature. But the science was actually much further developed at the outset than is the case for most successful therapies.

An Anxious Day

Were you nervous on the day of the trial?

Extremely. Even though the event itself was very anticlimactic. I mean, hanging up a bag of blood cells and intravenously dripping them into a patient happens ten times a day in that intensive care unit. And that's just one of many medical wards here, and we're just one of thousands of hospitals.

Didn't you worry she might die?

Not from anything related to the procedure. I did worry that she might get a blood clot in her lungs or develop some other rare, life-threatening condition during the trial, which would have been an absolute disaster. I mean, if the first patient died while genetically modified cells were going into her body, who would agree to be the second patient? It could have set gene therapy back a decade.

What are the indications that the gene treatment helped?

At this stage, there is every indication she is doing well. No, better than well—she is doing beautifully in every way we can measure she is improving. Her parents are delighted because she is no longer sick all the time. In fact, she's just been sick once and that was when the whole family came down with flu. She was the first to get better! Her parents couldn't believe it. They were still sick in bed and she was running around playing. They say she smiles and laughs a lot more than before. As far as laboratory measurements are concerned, her T cell count is normal for the first time in her life, most of her immune function studies are improving, and some are now in the normal range. And we can isolate gene-corrected cells making ADA directly from her bloodstream. She has never shown any serious side effects from any of the infusions. We could not be happier about the way things are going. Our second patient, a nine-year-old girl, has had two infusions. She is also doing very well and the first preliminary data on her appear to show that she is improving.

How many more patients are you going to treat?

That's Mike Blaese's decision, since he is the PI (principal investigator) on the protocol. But our plan is to add another patient at the end of the summer and maybe one more at the end of the year.

Risk of Cancer

Does the treatment carry risks for problems later on?

To introduce genes into the patient's cells, we use a vector derived from a retrovirus that can cause leukemia in mice. We snip out most of the retrovirus's genetic material so it can't cause disease, but there is always a remote possibility that when the new gene is inserted inside the patient's cells the process might cause cancer many years later.

Before the ADA trial, your group introduced a foreign gene into ten adults with advanced melanoma. The gene itself was not intended to have therapeutic benefits, so was this early trial done basically to show that gene transfer was safe?

In part, yes, since the risk to a terminal patient is almost infinitesimal. But another major motivation was to obtain information that could help medicine better develop cancer treatments in the future. Mike Blaese, our ADA expert at NIH [National Institutes of Health], saw that our gene transfer techniques could help Steve Rosenberg at NCI [National Cancer Institute], refine his new cancer therapy and got us all together. Rosenberg removes cancer-fighting white blood cells called TILs [tumor infiltrating lymphocytes] from the patient's tumor. In the lab those cells are multiplied ten-thousandfold using the growth factor interleukin-2. Then the TILs are given back to the patient. About forty percent of patients show at least a fifty percent reduction in tumor size. Ten percent have a complete response; there's no evidence of any remaining tumor.

For terminal patients, isn't that an incredible response?

Yes. But why does the treatment work for some and not others? Rosenberg needed some way to get a handle on what was happening inside the body. He needed to know where those TILs were going. What they were doing. That's where our technology could help. We tagged the TILs removed from the patients with a retroviral vector carrying a bacterial gene. When those gene-marked cells were returned to the body, they functioned a lot like a radio transmitter attached to a dolphin. We followed the TILs, saw how long they lived, where they went. It worked beautifully and perhaps has helped us to identify a subpopulation of lymphocytes more effective in fighting tumors. These findings may help us develop more powerful treatments against some types of cancer.

For example, Steve Rosenberg has already started treating two patients with advanced malignant melanoma by infusing TILs that contain the gene for tumor necrosis factor, an anticancer compound. Although it's too early to see any clinical response—we are still in the phase one safety trial—these patients have shown no toxicity from the gene transfer. Other approaches for using gene transfer to treat cancer are now being developed.

When did you know retroviruses would work in gene therapy?

By around 1983, I became convinced that they were the way to go. It was not a sudden revelation. I'd been talking with Ed Scolnick, then at NCI, about retroviral vectors since 1979–1980. But there were so many apparent problems with them. By late 1983, thanks to the work of [several scientists] I developed a deep instinctive conviction that retroviral vectors could be made to work in human gene therapy protocols.

Retroviruses normally carry genetic information into cells; that's how they reproduce themselves. They evolved to do just that, so they're much more efficient than micro-injection. With retroviruses we could get into millions of cells in one step, I should make it clear that I'm not the only person to have this idea. But, yes, most of the rest of the world thought we would never make it work in patients. Of course there were technical problems. There always are. But to me, the important thing was that I knew what ought to be done.

Relying on the Hidden Mind

Why are you so confident your experiments will work?

I've always had that ability. My conscious mind isn't so bright. I have trouble following lectures unless I know something about the subject. But when I get really interested in a problem, I take in all the information and totally immerse myself in it. My subconscious works on it all the time, and sooner or later it comes out. Sometimes I'll wake up at three A.M. with the idea for an experiment.

And it works?

Ninety percent of your "brilliant" ideas don't work the first time. And don't work for a long time—the experiment may drag on for months or years. Francis Crick once said if there's a conflict between theory and data, the theory's more likely to be correct. Most scientists think just the opposite, but I'm more like Crick. If an experiment ought to work, I'm convinced it will work, and stick with it until it does.

Injecting Genes to Curb Prostate Cancer

By Kambra McConnel

Gene therapy has shown itself to be a potential ally in the treatment of prostate cancer, according to Kambra McConnel in the following selection. The treatment employs gene therapy to stimulate cells in the diseased prostate to produce a natural substance called interleukin-2 (IL-2 for short). An injection pumps the genes directly into the prostate, and the resulting IL-2 summons killer cells from the immune system to its location. As Kambra McConnel reports, researchers believe that the killer cells then attack the tumor. As a result of a successful test conducted in May 2001 on twenty-four patients with advanced prostate cancer, researchers are convinced that gene therapy will prove less stressful than chemotherapy and more effective in curbing the spread of the cancer. McConnel was formerly a media relations officer at the Jonsson Cancer Center at the University of California, Los Angeles. She now holds a similar position at the University of Pittsburgh Cancer Institute.

R esearchers at UCLA's [University of California, Los Angeles] Jonsson Cancer Center have shown for the first time that immunotherapy delivered via gene therapy may prove to be a potent weapon in the fight against locally advanced prostate cancer, according to an article published Sunday (May 20) [2001] in the peer-reviewed journal *Human Gene Therapy*.

Lead author Dr. Arie Belldegrun, chief of urologic oncology at the Jonsson Cancer Center, said his early phase study suggests that intratumoral immunotherapy, in combination with surgery to remove the prostate, represents a new option for treating men with cancer that has spread beyond the boundaries of the prostate.

Historically, prostate cancer was believed to be resistant to immunotherapy. Belldegrun said his study proves otherwise.

"Based on our earlier studies in the laboratory, which were published in the journal *Cancer*, we suspected that this approach might work in humans," he said. "We did not know, however, that gene therapy and immunotherapy could be options for patients with locally advanced prostate cancer, a high-risk group to whom we have little to offer right now."

The study outlined in the article involves injecting gene-based immunotherapy—using an ultrasound guidance system—directly into the diseased prostate prior to surgery or after the failure of radiation therapy.

The treatment proved to be safe and, because the therapy was injected into the prostate and not delivered systemically, as chemotherapy is, it resulted in few side effects, Belldegrun said. And in more than half of the patients, the therapy resulted in reduced PSA levels, a blood marker that signals the presence of prostate cancer.

"This is the first clinical study of its kind aimed at exploring the role of immunotherapy and gene therapy in prostate cancer patients," Belldegrun said. "We're encouraged by the significant reductions of PSA levels and by the clinical outcome in this high risk group of patients."

In this study, 24 patients with locally advanced prostate cancer were treated with gene-based immunotherapy. A gene that expresses interleukin 2 (IL-2) was injected directly into the prostate.

A hormone-like substance, IL-2 stimulates the immune system to attract so-called "killer cells" called lymphocytes, which researchers hope will seek out and destroy cancer cells, Belldegrun said. The study proved for the first time that IL-2 is active against prostate cancer.

Belldegrun and his team of researchers use gene therapy to deliver the IL-2 to the prostate, a novel approach in prostate cancer. The IL-2 is a passenger of sorts, riding in the gene therapy vehicle, Belldegrun said.

The injection itself is done on an outpatient basis, so no hospital stays are necessary. The use of ultrasound for guidance allows researchers to deliver therapy with great accuracy.

"We proved this is a feasible approach for patients with locally advanced prostate cancer," said Dr. Robert Figlin, an oncologist at UCLA's Jonsson Cancer Center, co-author of the study and a professor of medicine and urology at the UCLA School of Medicine. "Because of its location, we were able to inject into the prostate these genes that stimulate the immune system to fight cancer. We anticipate that, in the near future, newer and more powerful agents will be delivered directly to the prostate via gene therapy—perhaps eliminating the need to remove the prostate. This is an important new concept and a proof of principle that the technology can work."

Because of the success in this early study, five centers nationwide, including UCLA's Jonsson Cancer Center, are now testing this treatment method in much larger phase II studies, Belldegrun said.

"We are encouraged by these early results and consider them valuable, especially in light of the apparent safety and lack of toxicity seen with this treatment," the *Human Gene Therapy* article states. "These results provide the foundation for the principle of locally administered gene therapeutic modalities in the treatment of prostate cancer."

If prostate cancer is discovered early enough, surgery is often all that's needed to eliminate the cancer. But when patients are diagnosed after the cancer has spread beyond the prostate, options are limited and survival rates decrease, Belldegrun said.

The difficulty is that early stage prostate cancer often results in few symptoms, so patients may not know they have the disease until after it has spread. In advanced prostate cancer, symptoms can include trouble having or keeping an erection, blood in the urine, swollen lymph nodes in the groin area and pain in the pelvic area.

A Common Cancer in Men

Other than skin cancer, prostate cancer is the most common type of cancer found in American men, according to the American Cancer Society. About 198,000 new cases of prostate cancer will be diagnosed in the United States this year. About 31,500 men will die.

Although men of any age can get prostate cancer, it's most common in males over 50. Men should be screened beginning at age 50. Those at high risk—African Americans and men with family members diagnosed with prostate cancer at a young age—should be screened beginning at age 45.

Swapping Out Bad Genes to Prevent Mitochondrial Disease

By Nell Boyce

Genetic diseases are, by definition, inheritable. One of the most mysterious is mitochondrial genetic disease. In the selection that follows, science writer Nell Boyce describes how gene therapy now offers a way to swap out bad genes in the embryos of mothers who have known mitochondrial defects so that their children will not develop the disease. However, Boyce explains, this amounts to germ line therapy, affecting the heredity of all descendants in that line. Germ line therapy, she says, raises fears of designer babies and clones. So far ethical panels and regulatory agencies have not approved treatments for mitochondrial disease, although thousands of parents hope that they will. Nell Boyce reports on health and medicine for *U.S. News & World Report*. A former writer for the British magazine *New Scientist*, Boyce has been honored by the National Association of Science Writers with an award for young science journalism.

G ene therapy could fix a defective egg—but at what cost? When Sharon Shaw was 18, one of her eyelids began to droop. A surgeon corrected the problem, but doctors were puzzled about the cause of the affliction. As she got older, other mysterious symptoms began to appear—first debilitating muscle weakness, then heart problems, and more paralyzing eye defects. Finally, at age 35, she was given a diagnosis: She was suffering from a mitochondrial disease.

Nell Boyce, "A Mother's Legacy," *U.S. News & World Report*, vol. 130, April 9, 2001, pp. 52–53. Copyright © 2001 by U.S. News & World Report, Inc. All rights reserved. Reproduced by permission.

Mitochondrial diseases are baffling genetic disorders. They range from mild to deadly, can occur early in life or late, and have no cures and few treatments. They are named for the tiny organelles, scattered throughout every cell of the body, that convert food into energy. These power plants contain a small amount of DNA—distinct from the chromosomes in the egg's nucleus—that is only passed on from mother to child. Once detected, mitochondrial diseases put parents in a bind. Indeed, Shaw worries that her 2-year-old son, Liam, will suffer. Although he looks fine now, she says, if she had known about her disease early, "I would have never had a baby."

Taboos Stand in the Way

Taking risks. Not all parents make that choice. Because mitochondria only get passed on from the mother, some couples resort to egg donation, and some decide to adopt. But the drive to have a genetically related child is so strong, and knowledge about transmission of mitochondrial disease so murky, that others decide to conceive and simply hope the child will be spared. Now, however, scientists have a way to completely replace an egg's mitochondria with healthy ones. Whether agonizing parents will actually benefit from the method, however, has less to do with science than with societal fears surrounding two genetic taboos: "designer babies" and clones.

Mitochondria contain a few genes that are essential for life. So swapping diseased mitochondria for healthy ones would in effect be an alteration of the egg's hereditary material. What's more, changing DNA in an egg, sperm, or embryo—so-called germline genetic engineering—has long been controversial. No one has dared try it in humans, because altering human genomes could have unknown consequences for future generations that inherit the changes. But Jacques Cohen, a prominent fertility specialist at St. Barnabas Medical Center in West Orange, N.J., has manipulated human eggs in a way that brings new urgency to the debate. Writing in the journal *Human Reproduction*, Cohen's group claims to have created "the first case of human germline genetic modification resulting in normal healthy children."

Cohen didn't set out to break taboos. His clinic sometimes rejuvenates infertile women's eggs by injecting them with the interior liquid of a donor egg. The technique works, and 30 babies have been born worldwide. But here's the ethical rub: Every egg's inner liquid contains the microscopic mitochondria and their DNA. Cohen's team has now analyzed blood samples from two of these babies and found that they contain DNA from three people: the mother, the father, and the egg donor.

Cohen plays down any broader ramifications of this fertility work, saying it may technically be a germline genetic alteration but that mitochondria and nuclear DNA are like apples and oranges. "It's a really different story," he contends. Other experts agree. "It's an absurdity to think that you're doing germline gene therapy by transmitting mitochondria," argues Jamie Grifo of New York University Medical Center. After all, they contend, the genes that control most human traits—like eye color or intelligence—reside in the cell's nucleus. These are the kinds of genes that ethicists have in mind when they wring their hands over designer babies.

Mitochondria in the Ethical Mix

But other scientists dismiss that line of argument as semantic hair-splitting. "You cannot say that mitochondrial DNA is not part of the human genome," says Theodore Friedmann of the University of California–San Diego. "Of course it is." That view has a lot of support from people like Mark Frankel, a scientist and policy analyst who cochaired a panel on germline genetic engineering organized by the American Association for the Advancement of Science. The panel not only included mitochondrial manipulation on its agenda but concluded that such work should be restricted. Frankel says: "There is no running away from what [Cohen] has either hinted at or said expressly. . . . We have an explicit acknowledgment of this in a prestigious journal. Now what do we do?"

Indeed, Cohen's feat is a fait accompli, whether one approves of such tinkering or not. So, since children have already been born with mitochondria from a donor egg, why not do it intentionally, as therapy? Each year, more than 4,000 babies are born with mitochondrial diseases. One British scientist is already planning animal studies on mitochondria replacement, hoping to someday apply it to human eggs as treatment. The technique he is interested in, however, isn't exactly the same as Cohen's. If donated mitochondria were injected into a woman's egg, the diseased ones would remain, and the resulting child would have mitochondria from both mother and donor. He prefers an approach known as "nuclear transfer," which takes the mother's egg and removes the nucleus—with all of the woman's chromosomes—and puts that nucleus into a hollowed-out donor egg.

Cloning in Disguise?

The problem with this technique, in some ethicists' eyes, is that it's essentially the same lab method used in cloning, though it's not an attempt to make a carbon copy of an adult. An expert panel convened by the British government did not see egg-to-egg nuclear transfer as problematic and in fact issued guidelines . . . urging researchers to explore the technique for treatment of mitochondrial diseases. But the U.S. Food and Drug Administration has cautioned fertility clinics not to manipulate human embryos in any way that's even vaguely related to cloning. And any method of altering genes in babies is "more profound than just producing a healthy baby," says Frankel. "We need an open and public discussion before we allow this to go on in a hit-and-miss way by people in fertility clinics."

But for some parents, waiting and debating is a life-or-death matter. Jennifer DeMeo of San Diego has lost two sons to mitochondrial disorders. Her first child, Lee Jr., appeared normal at birth, but he developed slowly, never walking or talking before he died at age 5. Her second son, Jacob, died at 8 months. While the prospect of altering genes in eggs does give her pause, she thinks the therapeutic uses of genetic manipulation could and should be separated from concerns about designer babies. "I have no problem with changing the gene to make a healthy child," says DeMeo, who adds that what Cohen has done in creating a child with mitochondria from two women "kind of gives me a little hope that maybe technology could be coming quicker than I thought."

Helping Children Born Without Immunity

By Steve Connor

For those born with genetic defects or deficiencies, the advent of genetic therapies may be a lifesaver. In the following selection Steve Connor reports that one of the first spectacular successes of gene therapy was the lifesaving procedure that saved the life of a girl born without an immune system. Children with this type of genetic defect are so vulnerable to disease that their parents cannot even hug them for fear of transmitting a deadly illness, Connor explains. To save the life of a two-year-old Arab-Israeli girl named Salsabil, in June 2002 doctors removed some of her marrow, infused it with specially prepared viruses containing corrective genes, and then reinserted the marrow into her bones. Weeks later, Connor reports, doctors observed the beginnings of an immune response: White blood cells began to appear in her blood. Months later, he says, her body was warding off many of the diseases that had earlier threatened her life, and after a year her doctors declared her cured. Scientists around the world reacted with cautious optimism as reports of similar successes began to emerge. However, with many more failures than successes to its name, Connor says, gene therapy's future remains uncertain. Connor is science editor for the London-based newspaper *Independent.*

An International team of doctors passed another milestone in medical history yesterday [June 27, 2002] curing a two-year-old girl of an inherited disorder of the Immune system using revolutionary gene therapy.

The girl, an Arab-Israeli called Salsabil from Jerusalem, was born without an immune system and would almost certainly have died within months of birth without the treatment. Now she is normal and healthy, in effect cured of one of the most feared genetic diseases.

Her survival is living testament to the growing realisation that gene therapy may have come of age after many years of false hopes. Doctors throughout the world are growing increasingly confident about the future of gene therapy, a technique where "healthy" genes are injected into a patient to replace their defective DNA. Salsabil was born in February 2000 into a family with a history of a gene disorder known as severe combined immunodeficiency (SCID), often called bubble baby syndrome because victims must be kept in a sterile environment.

One of Salsabil's siblings had died of the disease and an older sister, Tasmin, had survived only after a transplant of blood cells from the umbilical cord of a younger, unaffected brother. Unfortunately for Salsabil, there were no suitable donors for either a bone-marrow transplant or for stem cells from the umbilical cord blood. At seven months of age doctors decided gene therapy was the only option.

Making Room for Healthy Marrow

The team was led by Professor Shimon Slavin, Shoshana Morecki and Memet Akar of the Hadassah-Hebrew University Medical Centre in Jerusalem. They worked with Claudio Bordignon and colleagues at the San Raffaele Institute for Gene Therapy in Milan.

Israeli surgeons extracted bone marrow from Salsabil and mingled the cells with a genetically engineered virus containing a healthy copy of the affected gene. The virus, engineered to be harmless, automatically injects the human gene directly into the nucleus of the bone-marrow cells.

Before the doctors transfused the bone marrow back into Salsabil, they performed a radical procedure to increase the chances of the technique working. They subjected Salsabil to a mild form of chemotherapy—called non-myeloblative conditioning—to suppress her defective bone marrow cells and prepare the ground for the transfused cells to multiply.

Dr Bordignon said: "Non-myeloblative conditioning means you don't really wipe out the bone marrow, you just give one of the drugs used for a transplant, at a much lower dose, to make space for engineered marrow to seize, expand and grow better."

It worked. Within weeks of having a transfusion of her own marrow, Salsabil began to show signs of recovery. The infused stem cells migrated naturally to her bone marrow and began making several of the key cells of the immune system, such as the white blood cells known as B and T lymphocytes. Within months, Salsabil began making her own antibodies for the first time, when before she had to rely on those in her mother's milk. She responded normally to a tetanus vaccine and even survived chickenpox.

Within a year she had shrugged off the respiratory infections, chronic diarrhoea and scabies that had plagued her since birth. She was allowed home and needed no treatment. She was effectively cured of a disease written in her genes.

Declaring Victory

"I would call this a cure," Professor Slavin said. "We have achieved 100 per cent replacement of her defective bone marrow cells. She is a cute little girl. The concept can be applied to all genetic diseases where there is a need to engineer stem cells to produce normal products, especially when patients have no matched donor available for safe bone marrow transplantation."

It is not the first time that doctors have cured SCID children with gene therapy, but it is the first time a child has been cured of such a complex form of the disease. Salsabil suffered from a lack of an enzyme called adenosine deaminase (ADA), which results in a number of abnormalities of the immune system and is considered the most complex and most difficult SCID to treat.

W. French Anderson of the University of Southern California, who was the first to try to treat ADA deficiency by gene therapy, said yesterday the Italian-Israeli study was an important advance for the entire concept of gene therapy.

"This gives a boost to the whole field because it proves our basic premise, that if you can get enough gene-engineered cells into the patient it will cure the disease," he said. "That is very important and this is very exciting."

A Shaky Past

It was not always so. After the initial hype that heralded the first gene therapy attempt by Dr Anderson in 1990, the prognosis did not look good. Gene therapy alone did not cure in the way it was meant to and two little girls—Ashanthi deSilva and Carly Todd, the first gene therapy patients in America and Britain, respectively—had to rely on more conventional treatment to survive.

"There was initially a great burst of enthusiasm that lasted three, four years where a couple of hundred trials got started all over the world," Dr Anderson said. "Then we realised that nothing was really working at the clinical level."

The worst moment came in September 1999 when an American patient called Jesse Gelsinger died after a gene therapy injection into his liver. No one knows for certain why he died, but it may have been linked to the virus used in the experimental procedure.

It was a development that was carefully monitored by Britain's gene therapy advisory committee, experts responsible for overseeing all UK gene therapy trials. Scientists had to redouble their efforts to ensure the safety of any viruses used in the many and varied trials, which included attempts at treating cancer with genetically modified cells as well as treatments for some of the 4,000 or so inherited disorders caused by a single defective gene, from cystic fibrosis to haemophilia.

Signs of Success

Finally, in April 2000, scientists in France reported their first unequivocal success with gene therapy—on children with another form of SCID. This year [2002], doctors at the Institute of Child Health at Great Ormond Street Hospital in London reported similar success on an 18-month-old called Rhys Evans who had an SCID caused by a defect in the "gamma c" gene.

Today Rhys is a healthy two-year-old with no signs of the inherited disorder that had confined him to the solitary world of an antiseptic hospital room. Like Salsabil, he mixes freely with other children—an activity that might have killed them both before the treatment—and he now lives the normal life of any toddler. Adrian Thrasher, the consultant immunologist at Great Ormond Street who treated Rhys, said the research from Jerusalem was very encouraging for the treatment of immunodeficiency by gene therapy. He hopes the treatment may now be extended to cover other inherited illnesses. "There are more than 4,000 genetic conditions, and at least 80 different immune diseases alone," he said. "The technique will have to be worked out for each individual condition."

Treating diseased cells in the bone marrow is technically easier than treating the defective genes of, say, nerve tissue or heart muscle.

Although gene therapy has now proved effective in curing one or two diseases, nobody can yet be sure that such treatment can be made to work in each of the thousands of genetic disorders affecting children.

Treating Deafness with Gene Therapy

By Michael Hoffman

While artificial implants have succeeded in restoring hearing to some people, gene therapy offers the possibility of regrowing the capacity for hearing from within. As Michael Hoffman reports in the selection that follows, scientists at the University of Michigan have taken important first steps in the effort to restore hearing. The key, according to Hoffman, is to replace special hairs that transmit vibrations to other parts of the ear. Once these auditory hairs are lost, he says, deafness inevitably follows. Until recently, all attempts to coax the hairs to regrow have failed. However, in 2003, the University of Michigan researchers succeeded in using gene therapy to make auditory hairs grow in the ears of guinea pigs. The researchers found that neurons began to grow toward the new hairs in what they took to be a promising sign of hearing restoration. All the same, Hoffman says, much work remains to be done, and it could be a couple of decades before the technique can be made available to the public. Hoffman reports on medical matters for the United Press International wire service.

University of Michigan researchers say they have made a breakthrough that could lead to new treatments for human deafness and age-related hearing loss—they used gene therapy to grow auditory hair cells in a mammal subject.

The hair cells, found in the inner ear, are connected to a tuning membrane, which in turn is connected to sensory neurons that conduct sound waves directly to the brain. Although some people are born without these hairs, a condition that causes deafness, many people also suffer a loss of these hairs from infection, aging, exposure to loud noises and certain medications.

Michael Hoffman, "Gene Therapy Could Treat Deafness," *UPI Science News*, May 31, 2003.

"The loss of hair cells is irreversible, along with the deafness caused by it," said Yehoash Raphael, an associate professor of otolaryngology at the [University of Michigan] Medical School in Ann Arbor.

Although research done during the late 1980s proved gene therapy could be used to grow non-sensory hair cells in the ears of chickens, until now, scientists have been unable to grow auditory hair cells in mammals. This demonstration, Raphael said, brings the possibility of achieving auditory hair cell growth in humans.

Raphael and colleagues used adult guinea pigs to implant a gene called Math 1 surgically into the animals' inner ear fluid. The Math 1 gene is an embryonic gene, which determines the type of a premature cell.

After implantation, auditory hair cells began to grow in previously hairless areas of the guinea pigs' inner ears. The researchers also found evidence that sensory neurons began growing toward the hair cells.

The additional development is critical, Raphael explained, because without connection to the neurons the hair cells are useless. However, he added, the research has yet to demonstrate that the neurons and hair cells have achieved normal connection and function.

More than 30 million Americans suffer from hearing impairment and the new approach could be a major step toward restoring their sense of sound, said Doug Cotanche, associate professor of otology and laryngology at Harvard Medical School in Cambridge, Mass.

"Until now gene therapy has not worked that spectacularly in the ear," he added.

Far to Go

Cotanche said the next step in the research will be growing auditory hair cells at specific locations in the ear to stimulate the sense of sound. Although the UM team grew hair successfully in the inner ear, the auditory hair cells need to grow directly on the inner ear organ called the cochlea. This is the snail-shaped tuning membrane of the ear connected to the sensory neurons.

The fluid surrounding the cochlea stimulates movement of tiny projections of the hair cells. This creates electrical signals that are picked up by auditory nerve fibers and carried to the brain.

A surgical process called cochlear implantation already exists that can safely restore a child's or person's ability to hear. From 70 percent to 80 percent of infants who receive the surgical process and finish proper rehabilitation can attend normal schooling, said Dr. Daniel J. Lee, a pediatric cochlear surgeon at the University of Massachusetts Memorial Medical Center in Boston.

However, "it would be great if you could reverse or prevent hearing loss with gene therapy so they would not need a cochlear implant," Lee said.

Susan Fiorillo, of Worcester, Mass., has a 12-year-old son who would benefit from the gene therapy treatments for exactly this reason.

Her son has lived with hearing loss since his birth and it has progressively gotten worse with time. At a young age he received the cochlear transplant, but due to surgical complications he lost his hearing completely in one ear.

Another surgical implantation of a new cochlear was done successfully last April [2002] on Fiorillo's son's other ear, but nothing could be done for the surgically damaged one.

A Mother's Hope

"I'm not sure yet about the potential complications of gene therapy, but if it is proven to be safe I would much prefer the growth of healthy hair cells," Fiorillo said. "He lost that one ear forever and it would be wonderful if he would have two good ears instead of one."

Cotanche cautioned, however, that clinical use of gene therapy is still 20 years away. The research is in its preliminary stages and before the treatment could go into clinical use it would need testing on humans and approval by the Food and Drug Administration, he said.

In addition, the danger of side effects remains. The gene therapy performed on the guinea pigs resulted in damage to the animals' cochlear organ.

A New Tactic to Fight Parkinson's Disease

By Michael Kaplitt and Theodore Friedmann, interviewed by Ira Flatow

In this interview conducted by Ira Flatow, which was taken from a National Public Radio call-in program transcript, surgeon Michael Kaplitt explains how his team has used gene therapy for the first time in August 2003 to fight Parkinson's disease. Unresponsive cases of the neurological disorder, he explains, are usually treated by inserting an electrode deep into the brain and stimulating a certain area. Kaplitt, who is professor of neurological surgery at Weill Cornell Medical College, says his team followed the same procedure, except that instead of electrical stimulation, they inserted specially prepared viruses loaded with genes that the researchers hope will cause the affected area of the brain to return to normal function. The genes are expected to stimulate production of a chemical compound known as GABA, which can temporarily relieve the symptoms of Parkinson's.

Theodore Friedmann, who chairs the National Institutes of Health's main human genetic experimentation oversight committee, commends the Kaplitt team for its innovative approach to Parkinson's disease but expresses concerns about whether Kaplitt's procedure has been tested sufficiently in animals. Friedmann regrets, for example, that no monkey studies have yet been published using the procedure.

ra Flatow, host: This week [August 2003] comes news of the first effort by researchers in New York and New Zealand to treat Parkinson's disease by inserting genes directly into the

Ira Flatow, "Analysis: Gene Therapy for Parkinson's Disease," www.sciencefriday.com, August 22, 2003. Copyright © 2003 by National Public Radio, Inc. Reproduced by permission.

brains of people with severe cases of the disease, and the first surgery was done this week. The neurosurgeon who did the operation is here to talk about it. He has been criticized by some observers who say this clinical trial is premature because the procedure, they say, has not been tested enough on laboratory animals to ensure its safety and efficacy. . . .

Let me introduce my guests. Michael Kaplitt is assistant professor of neurological surgery at the Weill Cornell Medical College and director of the Center for Stereotactic and Functional Neurosurgery at New York Presbyterian Hospital–Weill Cornell Medical Center here in New York. And he's here in our New York studios. Welcome, Dr. Kaplitt.

Michael Kaplitt (Weill Cornell Medical College): Thanks for having me.

Flatow: Theodore Friedmann is the chair of the Recombinant DNA Advisory Committee for the National Institutes of Health. He is also a professor of pediatrics, the Muriel Jeannette Whitehill chair in Biomedical Ethics, and the director of the Program in Human Gene Therapy at the University of California–San Diego, and he joins us today from the campus there. Welcome to the program, Dr. Friedmann.

Theodore Friedman (National Institutes of Health): Thank you very much. Happy to be here.

Injecting Genes into the Brain

Flatow: Thank you. Dr. Kaplitt, tell us, on Monday, you made the first attempt to treat Parkinson's with gene therapy. Can you give us a thumbnail of how you did that?

Kaplitt: Sure. What we did was we performed an operation that, in most respects, was identical to a standard operation that we do right now routinely for patients with Parkinson's disease who are no longer responding well to medical therapy or who have side effects from medical therapy. And what that entails is making a hole in the skull the size of a quarter and finding a spot deep in the brain that we can initially visualize on MRI or other advanced imaging technologies. And then we probe that area of the brain with fine electrodes while the patient is awake so that we can ensure that we can accurately identify this very tiny structure and operate in the right space.

Now normally at that point, what we would have done is put in a stimulating electrode that we would attach through a wire to a battery in the chest, and this is called deep brain stimulation. And this is current standard surgery for Parkinson's disease.

Flatow: And gene therapy then is—well, you took the genes— were these his own genes or what ha. . .

Kaplitt: Right. So at this point, instead of putting in the electrode. . .

Flatow: Right.

Kaplitt: . . . we injected into the same spot these viruses that contain a copy of a human gene that will essentially change the function of the cells in this area of the brain and try to make them function in a way that would be more like a normal brain.

Flatow: And how do you get the genes to go where you want them to go?

Kaplitt: Well, first, by where we inject them using this technique so that we're putting this very fine tube or catheter roughly the size of a human hair into this area. And then we also ensure that the gene could actually efficiently get into these cells using these modified viruses, since viruses have evolved over millions of years to be very efficient, nature's gene-delivery vehicles essentially. . . .

We have tried over the years to do as much as possible to, first and foremost, worry about safety before we would consider going to human patients. My colleagues and I, particularly my colleague Matt During, who has helped develop this along with me, have been working in this field for 15 years, and we've been specifically working on this particular vehicle, the so-called adeno-associated virus, for over 10 years. We have experience not only in our own labs, but there have been many other labs working with this vehicle over that period in literally thousands of rats and numerous monkey studies. Both before this trial, as well as in support of this trial, we had a monkey safety study that was presented to the RAC [Recombinant DNA Advisory] Committee, as well as to the FDA [Food and Drug Administration], where we followed these monkeys for over a year.

Our RAC efficacy data was published in *Science* magazine this past fall, in October [2002], and those animals were followed for an extensive period of time. In none of the rats and in none of these monkeys that we had followed for over a year did we see any evidence of damage to the brain, any behavioral problems, any evidence of toxicity. The only thing that we had ever seen was a transient fever in a couple of animals in the first 24 hours that disappeared. So after all of that, which was all presented publicly at the RAC meeting, which, by the way, is Webcast even so that anyone in the public can see these meetings, and then that was presented two and a half years ago, and then was subsequently presented to the US Food and Drug Administration, who analyzed this for over a year, then was reviewed by our institutional review board, our peer review board, at Weill Cornell, as well as at North Shore Hospital, where this is being carried out, as well as the data that I said that was published in *Science* magazine.

We felt that after all of this time that we were comfortable that safety was the first and foremost thing that we had demonstrated, even though there is always the caveat that this has not been tried in human beings, and that is the reason why this is a safety study.

Doubts About Long-Term Effects

Flatow: Dr. Friedmann, you find any problem with the studies that were done prior to these?

Friedmann: I think when the RAC reviewed the proposals, as Dr. Kaplitt said, we went back to him and to Dr. During with a whole series of recommendations for what we thought might be improvements in the study involving technical things, scientific questions, where does the virus go, what cells does it infect and what's the long-term consequence of that in an appropriate animal model, and that means, of course, rats and mice, but then in a monkey model, which is engineered to resemble real Parkinson's disease. And I think many of the criticisms that you've heard in the last few days really center around the fact that the general community, the general Parkinson's community and the scientific community, haven't seen these results in published form and, therefore, can't really comment on how faithful the model is in the monkey studies. And, of course, the time required for follow-up has been relatively short. So the Parkinson's community, I think, still has some concerns that the long-term consequences of this really quite imaginative and unique study are still not known and, therefore, there's still a safety question in the minds of people who are following the study. . . .

Kaplitt: I think people should be aware a bit about the concept behind this because there are additional safety measures that we have tried to address beyond simply doing what we believe is ex-

tensive animal safety testing in advance. In particular, the operation that we are doing is designed specifically to try to take advantage of what we know works best today in human beings, not
in animals. So as I mentioned, for patients with Parkinson's disease, one of their problems is that there's an area deep in the brain
that is abnormally active, and what we try to do to relieve those
symptoms is quiet that area down either by destroying the area,
so-called subthalamotomy, for example, or put in these deep brain
stimulating electrodes to electrically silence the area. So we know
silencing this area can have a benefit to patients, human beings
with Parkinson's disease today.

Now when you look at the circuit and the chemistry of that area,
one of the reasons why that area becomes hyperactive is because
there is a chemical being released from different parts of the brain
into that area, and it's a chemical called GABA, and that usually
acts as the brain's brake. It silences brain areas. And so what we've
decided to do is go into this area and put the gene in that will allow it to make its own GABA and quiet itself down more naturally, and try to re-establish the normal chemical balance that
should ordinarily be in this area of the brain.

A Fallback Option

Now as I just mentioned, one of the operations that is being done
in many places around the world right now is to destroy this area
of the brain. So if there was something to occur, for example, that
we have not yet seen in any of our animal studies, where there
would be a problem for making too much of this chemical, GABA,
one of the potential options that we could have would be to go back
into that same place and either put in one of these electrodes to try
to quiet that down or, in the extreme example, destroy this area, and
that is a treatment that is being done right now in human patients
for Parkinson's, and that would destroy the source of this GABA
production. So we have even tried to build into this protocol measures that would give us options, even for those things that could
happen that we have not seen in any of our animals.

Flatow: Well, why not wait till after you've published the monkey data to make people, you know, less wary that you're going
ahead with this groundbreaking—I think everybody will agree it's
a groundbreaking surgery—to wait for that to come out?

Kaplitt: Well, first of all, like we said, we waited for the *Science* paper to come out with our rodent data. I think it's a bit unclear at best whether primate efficacy data—and our data will be coming out and be published, but whether primate efficacy data actually has any real bearing on success or failure in human patients, for example. There was some very nice positive results from primates with fetal cell transplantation and, of course, that's been a difficult human study. Deep brain stimulation that I just mentioned, which we are using in human beings right now, has not been tested in primates. So I don't know whether there is real clear evidence that success or failure in primates really defines success or failure in human beings, but we felt comfortable that we had extensive efficacy data in our rodents, the results that will be coming out on our primates, and we have extensive safety tests where we felt comfortable that this would be a reasonable thing to do.

Flatow: Dr. Friedmann, anything wrong with this logic?

Friedmann: Well, I would like to push it a little further, and in conversations with my neurological and neuroscience friends, I hear the argument very often that, of course, the rat, the rodent is not wired in the same way as a primate brain, and that what you see in terms of both safety and the overall effect on the global function of the brain in the rat cannot be extrapolated quite very easily to the primate and to the human. The brain functions in very interactive and very sort of highly orchestrated and choreographed and finely tuned pathways, and if one were to disrupt any one of those pathways, then the chances of wreaking havoc in the brain are fairly good and not necessarily detectable in rodent studies.

I mean, we've learned that, as Dr. Kaplitt said, from the more or less failure of the fetal implant studies and the great promise now of the stem cell approach, although we're likely to run into unforeseen difficulties with that as well. I think Drs. Kaplitt and During are really to be commended for this different approach to Parkinson's disease. They've chosen a unique approach, but all the more reason to prove it to the hilt, and the natural stopping point before you go to the clinic is to pick absolutely the most relevant animal model that exists, and in this case, the most relevant model is really a damaged monkey brain that really mimics the Parkinson's phenotype, the Parkinson's situation. And as far as we can tell, at least from the literature and in presentations, the demonstration of real efficacy and safety long term in this animal model, in the parkinsonian monkey, is what's so glaringly absent in the discussions.

The Risk of High Expectations

And so we would all like to see that. We're all reminded, of course, about raising too many expectations with preliminary studies. The field of gene therapy has suffered from that in the past, and we certainly want to be sure that when we describe a potential new approach to therapy that we're really going to be able to deliver. And that's what we would all hope for.

Kaplitt: Well, I would simply add that the whole reason that we took this very approach, as opposed to many of the approaches that we and others have worked on over the years that we did not feel was ready for the clinic and that we did not pursue, is precisely because we felt that this was a more conservative and more rational approach to trying to safely bring gene therapy to the brain to provide some efficacy for our patients without in any way attempting to even promise a cure for the disease with this approach, because I personally think that when we attempt to overreach and try to promise cures or develop things and only put things in that represent cures, that sometimes we can either, on the one hand, inappropriately delay innovative therapies or, on the other hand, get into trouble with toxicity.

I would add that there is a published study in human patients where this chemical, GABA, was actually directly injected into this very area of the human brain in awake patients during standard Parkinson's disease surgery and that the area did quiet down and those patients' symptoms transiently improved while that chemical was there. And we also used that as part of our rationale. So based on our experience in human beings with quieting this area down, both electrically as well as injecting this very chemical that the gene would allow us to make, as well as based on the ability to have these backup measures to potentially protect a patient if there were potential problems. That was the whole genesis of this idea.

Flatow: And the patient was fully informed about the risks and . . .

Kaplitt: Oh, without question, absolutely. The patient had to not only sign a 30-page informed consent, but we spent numerous hours on several sessions, both at my own institution, as well as the neurologists, David Eidelberg and Andrew Fagan at North Shore Hospital and in Long Island, who are the ones who, by the way, are both recruiting patients as well as determining the outcome. They spent many hours as well with them explaining all of this. . . .

Flatow: Dr. Kaplitt, will we know if this was successful? How will we know if your . . .

Kaplitt: Well, there are several measures that we've built into this study. First of all, as I said, success or failure in this particular study is safety. That's the purpose of the study. So certainly, we will know if his symptoms don't significantly worsen any more so than one would expect for a natural progression of the disease. And if he does not develop any new neurologic or other problems, then we'll certainly know—and with other patients as well—that the safety angle will have been met.

We also have built in, of course, extensive clinical measures to see whether his symptoms changed at all over time, for good or bad, whether his medications change over time, extensive neuropsychological testing frequently, and then especially—which we think is one of the more attractive features of this trial—is we built in PET scanning, which is a non-invasive way to look at the functioning of the different areas of the brain that are affected by our potential gene therapy. And this is something that we also built into this monkey study that is currently being written up, and so we have tried actually to test this in the preclinical setting as well. But this way, we have already, for example, scanned this particular patient in advance of surgery, and he'll get these regular scans over time.

Hope for Victims of Lou Gehrig's Disease

By Carey Goldberg

Gene therapy shows promise in treating a deadly disease that attacks the nervous system. The disease, amyotrophic lateral sclerosis (ALS), commonly called Lou Gehrig's disease, kills motor neurons, leaving victims progressively crippled and eventually unable to breathe on their own. To date, no treatment has been successful against ALS. In the following selection, however, journalist Carey Goldberg reports that researchers at the Salk Institute and Johns Hopkins University achieved "striking results" with gene therapy in mice in August 2003. Using specially engineered viruses, the researchers directed genes into the central nervous systems of the ALS-stricken mice, where they produced a substance that helped keep motor neurons alive, Goldberg says. Mice who received the treatment reportedly lived as much as 50 percent longer than they would have otherwise. Although gene therapy is not a cure, it offers so much promise for delaying the ravages of ALS that researchers and patient advocates want to proceed to human trials as soon as possible, according to Goldberg. Goldberg reports on health and other matters for the *Boston Globe*.

Scientists yesterday [August 7, 2003] said they had found the most effective treatment yet for lab mice with Lou Gehrig's disease, a fatal nerve disorder that afflicts 30,000 Americans, and researchers at Massachusetts General Hospital said they hoped to start trying the technique in humans in about a year.

The treatment relies on gene therapy, which has been known to cause serious, even fatal, complications in humans.

Nevertheless, the results in mice are so striking, and the disease—formally known as amyotrophic lateral sclerosis, or ALS—is so terrible that human trials are justified, researchers and patient advocates said. They also noted that the virus to be used in the gene therapy has a good safety record.

"There's not one effective treatment for this uniformly fatal disease—it's just crazy," said Valerie Estess, research director of Project ALS, a nonprofit group that largely financed the research.

A Paralyzing Disease

ALS attacks the motor neurons, nerve cells that control movement, but usually leaves thinking processes intact, so patients find themselves trapped inside a body that slowly loses the ability to move, to speak, even to breathe.

Death generally comes in two to five years, though with exceptions, like the famous theoretical physicist, Stephen Hawking, who has had the disease since college and is now 61. Lou Gehrig, the baseball superstar after whom the disease is named, died of it in 1941 at age 37.

The new therapy, published in the journal *Science*, slowed the degeneration in mice that had been genetically altered to have ALS, and extended their maximum life span to 265 days from 140 days.

Researchers at the Salk Institute and Johns Hopkins University injected the so-called adeno-associated virus into the legs and torsos of the mice. The virus had been engineered to carry a gene for "insulin-like growth factor-1," which can fight the neuron-killing effects of ALS. The virus migrated right into the central nervous system, a notoriously difficult target.

The technique "provides a novel way of delivering potent therapy directly to the heart of the disease—the dying or at-risk motor neurons in the spinal cord," said one researcher, Dr. Jeffrey Rothstein, director of the Packard Center for ALS Research at Johns Hopkins.

Drugs and another gene therapy have shown some effect in mice with ALS, Rothstein said, but they have generally been administered when the mice were babies; this latest therapy worked even when it was given to adult mice with ages parallel to the adult ages at which humans come down with ALS.

Still, he cautioned, even in mice, "It's not a cure."

Human Trials Are Next

Plans are already underway for initial safety tests of the new gene therapy in human patients at Johns Hopkins and Massachusetts General Hospital. The rough timetable is to get them going in a year or so, said Dr. Robert Brown, director of the Day Neuromuscular Research Laboratory at MGH.

"As the day approaches, we'll be looking for candidates," Brown said.

Gene therapy remains controversial, acknowledged Fred H. Gage, another author of the paper published in *Science*. But whether the treatment will work in humans "can only be determined by doing human experiments," he said. To run trials on humans, the researchers must get approval from the Food and Drug Administration; so far, researchers said, the agency has been easy to work with and shown deep awareness that ALS is an otherwise hopeless disease.

With an estimated 5,000 people diagnosed with ALS each year, there are likely to be many volunteers for trials.

Dr. Mickey McGrath, a 52-year-old doctor in Troy, N.Y., who has ALS, said he is confident the gene technique could stop the progression of his disease. He learned two years ago he has ALS, and these days walks with a walker and breathes with the aid of a tracheotomy tube. Speaking through his wife, Aileen, he said in a phone interview he is not worried about possible side effects of gene therapy.

"He doesn't think the side effects could be as bad as the disease," she said.

Gene Therapy and Immortality

By Susan McCarthy

Susan McCarthy reports in the following selection that some researchers think gene therapy can be used to prevent—or at least delay—death. McCarthy reports that scientists have used gene therapy on animals to block cellular self-destruct proteins and switch on genes that produce life-extending substances for cells. Gene therapy—or drugs derived from gene therapy—may provide a way to halt or even reverse the symptoms of aging, some scientists say. Gene therapy may even play a role in regenerating worn-out body parts. The more optimistic among researchers suggest that science may one day be able to engineer immortality. However, McCarthy says, there are practical and ethical problems to consider if gene therapy were one day able to make people immortal. If immortality, or something approaching it, becomes possible, she points out, there will be difficult questions to answer about who gets to live forever, and how to make room for more people on earth. McCarthy is a freelance writer and coauthor of the book *When Elephants Weep: The Emotional Lives of Elephants.*

One of the pleasing prospects that's ballyhooed as a future benefit of the Human Genome Project is increasing human longevity. The trouble with longevity is that if you go waltzing far enough down the path of long life you might find that you have merged with the highway of immortality without stopping at the weigh station of wisdom. Is that a perfectly good thing?

Can longevity extension go past combating diseases and address the very process of aging itself? If not, longevity will be less attractive. If, on the other hand, we can stay forever young, we may never want to leave the party. Should all of us be allowed to hang around as long as we want? Even creeps?

Research that may bear on the practical end of these matters is proceeding with startling speed.

Dr. Francis Collins, director of the National Human Genome Research Institute at the NIH [National Institutes of Health], told the *Washington Post* that within 30 years we'll know all the genes involved in the human aging process.

He cited an experiment in which manipulating one gene in a mouse extended the mouse life span by 30 percent. "Without manipulation, it seems that the maximum human life span is about 100 years. It is possible that could be extended if we understand the pathways of aging better," he said. He added that there are many ethical questions "that would have to be addressed before applying this on a broad scale." (I know people who already wish to sign up for the narrow scale.)

Disabling the Self-Destruct Switch

The elderly mice in question are Italian, and were engineered to be deficient in p66shc, a protein that tells a cell to self-destruct when it has sustained too much damage from free radicals (molecules produced throughout the body in the process of oxygen metabolism). This is thought to be a defense against the possibility that the damaged cells will become cancerous. But without p66shc, the mice live 30 percent longer. (Being mice, whose lives are brief, this means a few extra months of mousy joys.)

Dr. Huber Warner, director of the biology of aging program at the National Institute on Aging (NIA) is also optimistic about the Human Genome Project and the outlook for living longer. "The fruit-fly genome has just been sequenced. Now, if you look at genes known to be involved in diseases, two-thirds of those genes are found in the fruit fly, including some very important genes that are tumor-suppressor genes."

NIA is investing millions in research to find genes in animals like fruit flies or mice "which when mutated or expressed differently will alter the life span of those species," says Warner. "Now if you can identify those genes in model organisms, then the sequence of the human genome will give you the information you need to begin to extrapolate. We will figure out ways to manipulate the genes in the model organism and it'll suggest how those genes can be manipulated in humans."

Focus on Maintaining Health

Organizations like the NIA and the American Federation for Aging Research emphasize that they are not interested in increasing life span so much as increasing "health span," the years people can live with vitality, dignity and comfort.

Another avenue age scientists are racing down is telomere research. Telomeres are tasteful strands of nonsense DNA that decorate ends of chromosomes. Each time a cell divides, a bit of the telomere is clipped off. Eventually, when the telomere is a mere buzz-cut stubble, the cell stops dividing. There's a way around telomere loss: an enzyme called telomerase, which adds on extra telomere each time it's snipped shorter, so that it stays the same length, and the cell is not signaled to stop dividing. *Scientific American* has said telomerase "may well be the elixir of youth."

Some human tissues that divide indefinitely, such as reproductive cells producing sperm and eggs, contain telomerase. So do cells in embryos, but the telomerase gene is inactivated in most cells after birth.

Reactivating telomerase could replenish lost cells. Warner mentions the possibility of restoring epithelial cells in the retinas to restore lost eyesight. Telomerase genes have been successfully reactivated in retinal epithelial cells grown in tissue culture, in work done at the University of Texas Southwestern Medical Center and the Geron Corporation. Geron has filed for patents on hTRT, the telomerase reverse transcriptase protein. Warner notes, "The problem with turning telomerase back on is that's one of the things that happens in cancer." Cancer cells are all about telomerase and unrestricted cell division.

Steven Austad is a zoologist who studies aging. In his lucid, engaging book *Why We Age*, he describes his study of opossums on a Georgia barrier island—Methuselah opossums who had smaller families, often bred two years in a row instead of one, and aged more slowly, living a whopping three years instead of two.

Austad notes that when we discover and examine genes in the human genome that can increase longevity, they may prove to come with trade-offs. "Of all these genes in these small animals [that extend longevity], none of them are ever found in nature. And they all have downsides. People have not been eager to investigate the nature of their downsides."

Cancer obviously could be a downside, as could altered fertility.

Austad says he's been snorted at by other scientists when he argues that we should study the cells of long-lived animals like whales and elephants instead of short-lived ones like mice and fruit flies if we want to understand how we might live longer. "Elephants contain about 40 times the numbers of cells we do, and whales as many as 600 times as many cells. Yet elephants and whales live, to a reasonable approximation, just as long as we do. Therefore, their cells must be 40 to 600 times *more* resistant to turning cancerous than our own. Could we perhaps learn something about cancer resistance from studying these cells?" he has written.

So far, Austad himself isn't working with elephants. Instead he's looking at parakeets. "They live up to 20-plus years," he says admiringly. "That's seven times as long as a mouse, and they're the same size. They have unbelievable resistance to oxidative damage . . . if we could somehow mimic that in humans. . . ."

So, downside or no, Austad also thinks findings from the Human Genome Project will help us increase human longevity. "We already know that there are some genes that are associated with longer life in animals. I think we'll find the [corresponding] genes in humans that have a small but measurable effect on how long we live. And it won't be too many years before we have gene therapy for all kinds of things. It hasn't worked too well yet, but that's just a technical problem."

Is there any theoretical limit that would keep increased longevity from becoming immortality? Warner says "There's no theoretical limit. There's a balance between constant damage and repair. It's like a car. Theoretically you should be able to keep a car going forever—not yours, maybe, and not mine—but if you keep replacing the parts the car could last forever. Maybe the individual could live forever."

"The only limit is that there is no such thing such as immortality because accidents still happen," says Austad. "The theoretical limit is human behavior, not human physiology. If teenagers didn't drive cars like crazy people, that would probably have more effect on life expectancy than curing cancer."

Dr. Leonard Hayflick takes a darker view of longevity research than many scientists do. Hayflick's view of significantly increased longevity is, basically, that it won't happen, it can't happen, and if it did happen it would be a bad thing.

Hayflick, a professor of anatomy at the University of California at San Francisco's school of medicine, is the author of *How and Why We Age*, and has been thinking about longevity for 30 years, ever since he discovered what's now called the Hayflick Limit. Until his research, it was thought that animal cells growing in tissue culture were immortal and could divide forever. In a series of meticulous experiments, Hayflick showed that normal cells in culture have life spans: They flourish and divide for a while, but after a certain number of generations, divide no longer and eventually die. The cell lines that do go on forever are cancer cells.

People fail to distinguish between curing disease and ending aging, Hayflick says. If all the diseases currently written on death certificates in developed countries were resolved, you could add perhaps at the most 15 years to human life expectancy. "And that's it. Period."

Aging itself will not be affected. "Aging is an inexorable process that begins at about the age of 30 in humans and continues indefinitely. If you resolve disease you then expose or reveal the underlying real cause of that vulnerability, and hence death."

Hayflick doesn't believe that we will be able to go beyond resolving disease to slowing or stopping the process of aging. You can replace parts all you want he says, but what will you do when you have to replace your brain?

Holding On to Youth

It's true that people object to aging as well as to death. Long life, while much admired, isn't sought after so much as long healthy life, or perhaps long youth. We want to be 100 years old *and* dewy fresh.

Dr. Pier Paolo Pandolfo, one of the scientists who studied the mice that live 30 percent longer, told the *New York Times* that a drug to block the self-destruct protein p66shc (the one the mice were engineered not to have) could be applied in the form of a cream to reverse wrinkling and blemishes on aging skin.

Can we have both long life and long youth? "I would say that there's no question about that," says Austad. "Most people would say that if you can't have better function there's no sense in keeping people alive."

It's increasingly easy to imagine replacing our parts, renewing our tissues, and rewriting our DNA. We would also need to fix our memories. They can hold a great deal, but never needed to hold an infinite amount of experience. Yet there are various ways we might deal with that, such as adding memory chips to our brains.

Or perhaps we'll even figure out how to get rid of unneeded, unpleasant old memories and provide room for delightful new memories. It'll be doable, eventually.

Evolution Favors Mortality

Is this really possible? I believe it is, though I'm not fool enough to suggest a timetable. To those who say it'll never happen, I say: Don't confuse "a hell of a long time" with never. I think rather highly of human ingenuity and biological science. I see no reason why we won't eventually learn how to live forever and to live forever young.

I think less highly of collective human common sense. (As Kay tells Jay in that brilliant philosophical [movie], *Men in Black*, "A *person* is smart. People are dumb. . . .") And so there's no reason to suppose we will handle this knowledge wisely.

Why aren't we immortal already? If it's so easy to turn on a gene here and turn off a gene there, why do we wear out and die? It's all about reproduction, of course. Once we've produced the next generation and gotten them on their feet, what happens to us is of no relevance to the future. People who have two children and live to be 100 are less successful from an evolutionary standpoint than people who have three children and keel over in their 50s.

So the impressive genes that allow people to reach 100 on a diet of bacon and beer are not favored by natural selection. (Although if the centenarians spend all their time calling up their great-grandchildren and asking when they're going to have babies and the great-grandchildren cave in and produce more children than they otherwise would have, that might favor those genes a bit.)

Still, it seems a little odd that there are no immortal species around. Quahogs live to be 200, but they probably feel that's not nearly long enough. Perhaps species of immortal animals would always be outcompeted by species of mortal animals, since mortal species evolve and acquire exciting new bells and whistles to repel insect pests, protect against disease and fool dinosaurs into thinking you wouldn't dream of eating their eggs.

If we stop dying will our species stop evolving? Not if we keep reproducing. Not everyone thinks we need to keep evolving. Many of us feel that we are already the pinnacle of perfection and that all our species needs to do is stay as sweet as we are. Others disagree.

Choosing for Ourselves

My friend Cynthia Heimel says she does not feel we are nearly finished evolving, and she is eagerly looking forward to an era when we have progressed to having just four toes on each foot. She says it is because little toes are no use and catch on the bed corner, but I believe she just wants to wear pointier shoes.

In the choice between living long and having kids, natural selection has always favored having kids. Now that choice will be up to us. Obviously if we choose to do both, the world will fill up with people to such an extent that we'll have to look for new planets.

We will ourselves become natural selection—unnatural selection if you prefer. Instead of allowing the ceaseless cherry-picking of the generations to get rid of our back problems, our impetuous driving habits and that pesky fifth toe, we will do it all at once with gene therapy.

Will everyone get to live forever, or will we make decisions about how long people get to live and when they have to stop?

This is one of the reasons Hayflick thinks increasing longevity is a dreadful idea. "I defy anyone to describe a scenario in which it would be a good thing," he says.

Hayflick told the *Savannah Morning News*, "If indeed we had a way of extending human longevity the probability is very high that therapy would be available to the rich and powerful. I don't know how you feel about the rich and powerful, but I can think of lots of them that I would not like to see live forever." For example, he notes, "I don't think that having Adolf Hitler around for the next 500 years makes much sense."

The Cost of Dodging Death

You know Fidel Castro isn't ready to die. And while I am under the impression that I have accepted my own mortality, I must admit that I don't accept the mortality of my loved ones. It's not that I want them to be immortal, it's just that I don't want them ever to die.

The fact that we spend such a huge proportion of our health budget in the last few months of our lives is testimony to this. (As my father remarks, "You can't tell what truly expensive way of living a little longer will be discovered.")

Spending money on gene therapy will undoubtedly be more popular than the feeble unappealing ways we have now of extending life span a little. You know, boring stuff like eating right, keeping fit, signalling your lane changes.

There are some things people won't do to live longer, after all. Yes, we'll slam down melatonin, DHEA and random antioxidants by the fistful just in case they slow aging. But almost nobody has leapt on the caloric restriction bandwagon (which holds that since rats on meager diets live longer, maybe we would too, so let's not eat anything at all every other day), because it's so unpleasant.

I have also heard men complain about how unfair it is that women live longer on the average. (Some of them will glare at a lady as if she'd been sprinkling free radicals on their salads.) Yet although it has long been known that castration can extend a man's life span by an average of 14 years, guys consistently pass on the chance to even the score.

Is it any more unnatural to use gene therapy to become more or less immortal, than it is to use [it to] prolong life in other ways? After all, during most of human history most children died as infants, women couldn't effectively limit how many children they gave birth to (and were far more apt to die in childbirth), and very few of them reached old age—yet hardly anybody objects to medical care to fight these causes of death.

But what all these changes amount to for our species is simply a movement along the spectrum from the kinds of species that have brief risky lives in which they produce as many progeny as possible—like mice—to the kinds of species that have longer lives during which they have fewer progeny, in whom they invest more parental care—like elephants. These life strategies are called r selection and K selection, and there's nothing so unusual about a species becoming more or less K-selected.

But among all the variously r- and K-selected creatures in the world, one thing seems constant: Everybody dies eventually. Immortality is something different.

Can Ethics Make a Difference?

Then there's the matter of addressing ethical conflicts before we proceed. The track record on this is not so great. Conferences are held and panels meet and people go right ahead and do what they want. And people really really want to live. "If it becomes possible, people will do it," says Steven Austad.

There are people worrying now about the way better health care is producing an unprecedentedly large population of older people, and the effects this has on medical spending, education spending, Social Security and the GNP. Oh, and the ballot box.

Well, they haven't seen anything yet. The world will fill up a lot faster if nobody dies.

Maybe we'll make people choose between living forever and having kids. If you're going to bring more people into the world, you'll have to be willing to leave it yourself on a reasonable schedule. Conversely, if you refuse to leave the party, you can't bring crashers. Of course, this would create an interesting two-tiered world full of crabby child-haters who think they know so much because they've seen it all and breeders speaking smugly about how they're being not only natural but also more evolved.

What about natural selection? It got us this far, didn't it? If immortality is a bad idea, won't nature take care of it? It might do just that, but not in a way we'll enjoy. Since natural selection is mindless and purposeless, it has no objection to dead ends and short-term successes. Eventually some species could come along which has all our excellences, plus the advantages of mortality, and it will eliminate us. Not if we can stop them first, of course, but eventually (and this is a very long run indeed) we will be out-competed. Will the new Lords of the Earth then turn to making themselves immortal? Very likely, but it won't be our problem. Mother Nature doesn't care, ahistorical, short-sighted fool that she is.

Perhaps in the far reaches of time, as one mortal species after another crushes species that have succumbed to the temptation of eternal life, a species will arise that will remain mortal, and will allow itself to change. Perhaps they will never be overthrown by another species. Perhaps they'll have a zoo, and we'll be in it, and we'll learn the full reality of a life sentence.

CHAPTER 3

The Road
Turns Bumpy

Gene Therapy Research: Juggling Business and Science

By Joshua Kurlantzick

The biotech business has lured many scientists out of universities, hospitals, and major corporations into private start-up companies. In the waning days of the 1990s, as the Human Genome Project neared completion, venture capital flowed into start-ups. That surge later slowed to a trickle as an economic recession set in at the turn of the century, leaving many young biotech firms struggling for cash.

In the selection that follows, Joshua Kurlantzick reports on three scientists who have been working on a promising new gene therapy that may revolutionize cancer treatment. However, after leaving their jobs to found a company called Intradigm (pronounced intra-dime), they soon learn how difficult it is to keep enough capital flowing in to keep a biotech company afloat. To raise additional venture capital, they often have to approach new investors who do not understand their research in the same way as their old backers did. As Kurlantzick reports, newer investors may pressure scientists to pursue research aimed at quick profits, even if that means throwing long-term research better suited to fight disease off course. Joshua Kurlantzick is foreign editor of the *New Republic*. He previously reported on trade and international economics for *U.S. News & World Report*.

Joshua Kurlantzick, "Beat the Clock," *The Washingtonian*, vol. 38, July 2003. Copyright © 2003 by Joshua Kurlantzick. Reproduced by permission.

Sitting in his bare office, dressed in the biotechnology uniform of sweater and jeans, Martin Woodle ponders his future.

Intradigm, the Rockville biotech company he cofounded, could run out of cash by the end of the year, leaving Woodle, who has invested much of his life in the firm, with just a stock of ambitious ideas and experiments.

"You can always worry that everything you've built will fall down around you, that the money will run dry," he says. "That's part of being a small company."

Is he concerned about the company's survival?

"A lot of good companies are not making it," he says.

Intradigm is on the verge of developing a cancer treatment that could help make chemotherapy obsolete.

Oncologists have tried for years to shrink tumors by battering patients with chemotherapy, which often damages healthy cells as it tries to kill tumors. Intradigm's founders think they can discover which genes produce the "messenger" proteins that allow tumors to grow, and then learn to incapacitate them.

Turning Off Tumors

To do so, the company's scientists inject mice with ribonucleic acid (RNA) that they've altered. If they alter it correctly, the RNA, when injected, will turn off certain genes in the mice, preventing the mouse cells from receiving information that would lead to a cancer-causing protein. This process is called RNA interference.

When RNA interference hits genes and inhibits tumor growth, Intradigm notes the gene the RNA worked on. Because mice are strong predictors of success with humans, mouse genes that appear important to tumor growth and that can be turned off by RNA indicate which human genes would be targets for cancer-fighting drugs.

Intradigm's founders believe they, or another drug company, can develop medications that would mimic the effects of RNA injections and stop tumors—a potentially momentous discovery. *Science* magazine named RNA interference the top breakthrough of 2002.

"I compare what we're doing to dealing with a band next door making a racket," Woodle says. "The band is the tumor. Chemotherapy burns down the house next door trying to shut the band up but killing many bystanders. Drugs that exist now to fight cancer are poor at targeting the tumor. They might shut up one instrument in the band—one component of the tumor—but it could be the quietest instrument.

"Our technology will allow doctors to get right at what makes the tumor grow without debilitating the other cells."

Shortage of Funding

The economic downturn of the past three years [2001–2003] has hit the biotech landscape hard. Even though biotech stocks have begun trending upward again, venture capital is still scarce.

Unlike other tech industries such as software or e-commerce, biotech start-ups haven't yet created many breakthrough products or world-class companies such as Microsoft. Many touted biotech drugs have failed in clinical trials because, industry insiders say, biotech firms didn't spend enough time on initial tests and because the Food and Drug Administration—gunshy from approving several drugs in the 1990s that turned out to have serious side effects—has become too conservative.

Cash-strapped states like Maryland that are running big deficits have become less willing to spend money helping local biotech industries.

Singapore, India, and Japan—which have had little success breaking the American stranglehold over information-technology sectors—have lavished government money on biotech industries. These countries have started taking market share from American biotechs and luring scientists away.

As biotech start-ups have failed to bring products to market and have been stymied by the FDA, venture capitalists and other investors have become reluctant to gamble on them. Investors are focusing on surer bets—on big drug companies that already have brought many products to market or on other sectors, says Victor Li, who manages a biotech fund at the Arlington investment bank Friedman, Billings, Ramsey & Co.

To stay afloat, Woodle and his coworkers have tried to revamp Intradigm. Some changes are minor—slashing the few perks that existed at a company where the coffee corner is instant Nescafé and a water boiler. Some are bigger: The lack of money has forced Intradigm scientists to spend days on the road like traveling salesmen, seeking potential investors.

Intradigm's staff worries that, to stay in business, they're being forced to reshape experiments to deliver results that might win new financing. In the process, they say they risk future discoveries.

When Intradigm was founded in July 2000, biotech was the debutante of Washington. In the 1990s, funding increases for the National Institutes of Health had drawn young scientists here from across the globe. Many left NIH to found start-ups in Montgomery County. By 2000, Washington had more life scientists than any other region in the country.

Meanwhile, the Human Genome Project—an effort coordinated by NIH to identify the genes in human DNA—focused the public, investors, and media on Washington's biotech industry.

Between 1995 and 2001, fascination with the Genome Project snowballed. Many scientists and laypeople believed it would be the Rosetta Stone of disease—as scientists identified genes, they'd unlock the secrets to fighting nearly all ailments. Start-ups began focusing on genomics—the study of genes' functions—as a means of developing drugs.

Areas of Rockville became known as DNA Alley. Maryland restaurants held biotech happy hours. Dating services catered to biotechies looking for mates who knew proteins weren't just part of the Atkins Diet.

The founders of two well-known developers of gene-related drugs, Human Genome Sciences and Celera—both based in Rockville—talked up genomics to audiences and journalists searching for a buzz-worthy industry as dot-coms tanked.

Forbes, Fortune, and *Business Week* touted biotech as the next hot investment. *Vanity Fair* dispatched reporters to industry conferences to check out rising biotech executives.

Amid this euphoria, Woodle and two other scientists at Novartis subsidiary Genetic Therapy—India native Puthupparampil Scaria and China native Patrick Lu—started the company in 2000.

"Novartis did not really let us come up with ways to use new types of gene technology," Scaria says. "We talked about our idea of using animals to find which genes code for tumor-causing proteins, but we couldn't do the research the way we wanted there— where you had the freedom to try out a range of new ideas."

The founders knew that as long as they remained at Novartis, they'd never convert their research into serious profits.

Success seemed possible. "In 2000 and early 2001, if you had a good genomics idea and understood how to sell it, you could find funding and be on your way," says Robert Eaton of MdBio, a nonprofit group that supports Maryland biotechs.

Intradigm's founders huddled through late-night bull sessions to choose a name that evoked science and hipness—not easy for a bunch of guys who Woodle admits "are pretty dedicated to our work—we're not big socialites."

Ultimately, they settled on combining "intracellular" and "paradigm."

Raising Funds Without a Product

As Woodle and his compatriots were naming their company, other area biotechs were raising cash. NIH provided Washington companies with more than $900 million annually in 1999 and 2000. Private investors followed, hiring scientists as advisers and even setting up funds devoted to biotech.

Though it admitted it wouldn't have a marketable product for years, Human Genome Sciences raised more than $1.8 billion in 1999 and 2000 and used some of the cash to build a corporate headquarters on 55 acres in Montgomery County. Other biotech companies followed it onto the Nasdaq.

In some ways, the industry benefited from the Internet crash, which pushed even more investors toward biotech.

It was a risk to leave a conglomerate like Novartis, but it seemed a manageable one. Lu and Scaria were reassured that they had Woodle, a budding industry superstar who became president and CEO of the young company. He was an innovative scientist—by 2000 he held six patents. He also had worked in management at a previous biotech job.

"Martin hadn't been to business school, but we felt he was knowledgeable about raising money and other commercial aspects," Scaria says. "We thought we had a great idea, and if we could show investors where we were going, we would naturally raise capital."

In July 2001, the company secured $1.85 million in series-A financing, along with commitments for another $1 million, from a group of investors led by Emerging Technology Partners, a local venture-capital company with deep roots in the Montgomery biotech industry.

After searching DNA Alley, Intradigm found a small space in a Rockville office park—doors didn't even have company names on them—that fit its budget. Intradigm furnished it sparingly—some staffers kept vats of chemicals in their offices—and began hiring.

By summer 2002, the founders exuberance had faded. Intradigm's animal experiments were showing promise, scientists were learning how to turn off genes that code for cancer-causing proteins, and Woodle was making plans to present the company's initial successes to science conferences. But biotech's landscape had changed.

Venture Capital Shrivels

Even innovative scientists with world-class ideas were perishing if they lacked blue-chip backers. The country's economic stagnation had made venture capitalists cautious: American companies raised $21 billion in venture financing in 2002—down from $41 billion the year before.

Investors and the media had turned particularly sour on biotech, since many life-sciences firms like Celera and Human Genome Sciences had made claims they couldn't justify and were unable to bring drugs to the market.

"Human Genome Sciences made the biggest mistake any player in a young industry can—overpromising," says John McCamant, editor of Medical Technology Stockletter. "The public did not totally understand biotech, and they were taking companies' word on some things. But after the overpromising, they stopped."

Meanwhile, the media jumped on biotech scandals such as the troubles at ImClone Systems, which involved rumors of insider trading by [television personality] Martha Stewart. She has since been indicted [and eventually convicted] for her alleged actions, even though ImClone's cancer-fighting drug, Erbitux, still seems to have potential.

"They probably teach this in business school," Woodle says, "but one shock I have had at Intradigm, running the business side, is how failures in the sector ripple through and hurt every company."

[The September 11, 2001, terrorist attacks] didn't help. As the government threw money at bioterrorism defense, federal support for genomics suffered.

"The antibioterrorism firm that used to be in the space next door to us moved out," Lu says with a wry laugh. "I guess they found something more luxurious."

Rockville, which a year before had been awash in gold, started spurting red. Human Genome Sciences lost more than $75 million in the third quarter of 2002. EntreMed—a biotech firm focusing on cancer—cut operating expenses by 60 percent late that year. Celera looked like a tornado had hit. After the company laid off 130 people in 2002, it hauled away trailers built to accommodate staff, leaving plywood debris across the company's campus.

"Biotech is a high-risk, high-return sector, and some investors got scared off by those risks and underestimated the amount of time biotechs need to get products to market," says investment banker Victor Li. "But if investment drops for years, in the long run we won't get those high returns—lifesaving drugs and treatments."

Doing Things on the Cheap

Intradigm was treading water. Already living frugally, employees faced further cutbacks. A chipped Ping-Pong table now functioned as the employees' main source of Friday-afternoon entertainment. Employees cut back on travel and pored over expense reports. Intradigm started searching for cheaper space and let attrition reduce staff. The founders called a round of company meetings on frugality.

"We emphasized to all our employees that everything we did had to be very entrepreneurial," Lu says. "They had to do everything themselves, even the most basic things."

The savings helped, but they hardly paid for Intradigm to continue conducting animal tests. When the founders began looking for new sources of revenue in summer 2002, they made little progress. By the end of the year, Intradigm didn't have enough cash reserves left to pay for a year of continuing operations.

"Although we'd had initial success raising money," Lu says, "we really weren't as savvy about how to find financing in a time when people were not coming to us."

The cash shortfall could prove deadly. Most financial experts advise start-ups to maintain enough cash to pay for at least two years of operating expenses.

Says McCamant: "Not saving cash when you have the chance can separate start-ups that live and those that die."

By early fall 2002, Intradigm realized it had to bring in someone with more business experience.

Bringing in a Heavy Hitter

John Spears was a biotech executive with decades of experience running the business side of young companies and serving in management at Bristol-Myers Squibb, Ayerst Laboratories, and other conglomerates. He was hired as chairman and CEO in November.

Says Woodle: "We needed someone who could be the link between Intradigm and the outside world."

To prepare Intradigm to search for more venture-capital money, Spears helped refine Woodle's explanation of the company's science into snappier arguments that focused on differentiating Intradigm's technology.

"Martin had learned how to sell to investors in the first round of financing," Spears says. "But now that the economy was tougher, we had to do a better job of showing how we would meet goals in only months or years."

Spears began exploring new ways to raise capital. At industry conferences and trade shows, he approached pharmaceutical companies, asking whether they might want to license Intradigm's discoveries, which could help the larger companies with their drug development. He started considering collaborations with other biotechs and contacting potential investors in regions Intradigm hadn't explored—Europe, Asia, Canada. Intradigm had already signed a collaborative research-and-development agreement the previous winter with DirectGene, another local biotech (now called Advagen).

To help Spears, Woodle and the other founders conceded that, in the next round of capital-raising, they would give up a considerable amount of their original stock.

"With many start-ups, the founders can't conceive of giving original stock, because the company is their baby," Spears says. "Here, there's never been a question—these guys want to do anything that helps Intradigm survive."

Most important, Spears convinced the staff they had to perform fewer, less frequent experiments.

"The reagents that go into one of our experiments are expensive," Spears says. "The animals are expensive. Staff time is expensive. We have to get in a position where we have a couple years of cash in the bank. We have to be more selective, focus on using the experiments to meet shorter-term goals we can present to investors."

By January, Spears's hiring had galvanized some of the staff, but the business pressure worried many.

"We have a defined business plan for the next two years," Lu says, walking around Intradigm's offices, pointing out where the company might put new staff if it had money to expand. "We know where we're going."

Spears rattles off goals: The company will contact at least 50 venture-capital firms and other investors over the next six months. By late 2003, Intradigm hopes to have at least one venture capitalist committed to providing new capital, allowing the company to bank several years' worth of cash reserves and hire as many as 20 people.

Intradigm still retains a lead over competitors, though other biotech companies such as Massachusetts-based Sequitur and Australia-based Benitec have begun RNA-interference research. A year ago, Intradigm scientists pulling long nights made a crucial breakthrough, which they celebrated in true start-up fashion— by collapsing with fatigue. At the American Chemical Society's 2002 conference, Woodle showed that Intradigm had succeeded in turning off a mouse gene that might code for a tumor-creating protein—the first time RNA interference had worked in a living being. If the company can raise more cash, Spears says, Intradigm might be able to progress to human testing within two years.

Little Time for Research

But even as Intradigm was developing these plans and wowing conferences, the company questioned the bargains it was accepting. Preparing to push for a second round of cash, Woodle began spending hours with Spears to develop their pitch to venture capitalists.

Woodle says he's spending 50 percent of his time raising money, 40 percent on other business-development responsibilities, and only 10 percent on research: "It's obviously a balance I would like to change."

Watching their cofounder juggle his time, other employees wonder about the long-term impact of taking Woodle out of his natural habitat.

"We need Martin to be as involved as possible in the animal research," Lu says, "because he has a ton of insight."

In searching out so many sources of revenue from outside the region, Intradigm's principals risk finding the wrong investors— people who don't understand their goals, who might force the company to focus too much on the short term, who might challenge their integrity.

"The venture capitalists we started with in 2001 understand

genomics," Spears says. "You walk into their offices and you
face people with PhDs in life sciences, people who can grill you,
who are willing to give you a longer leash, to forgive some early
failures."

Would venture capitalists in Japan, Germany, or even San Jose
prove as forgiving?

"You have to strike a balance between long-term and short-term
goals," Woodle says. "We want to make money, and we want to
make money for our investors. But if you let business concerns
overshadow science too much, your experiments can get off-track.
Then ultimately everyone would lose—you won't be able to develop the kind of breakthroughs that would make money for investors and the company.

"Some new investors may want us to show that we're meeting
targets more frequently, and we might have to make our experiments shorter and cheaper. That's fine, but you wonder if you're
shortchanging your ability to take advantage of all the opportunities the research is opening up."

Most worrisome to staff, cutting back on experiments could ex-
acerbate the focus on short-term targets and prevent the company
from exploiting its brainpower advantage.

"Having people look at what's needed to do and what's not
needed to do can be healthy for any business," Spears says. "But
we might fall off our timetable for getting into human trials."

"The best way to build a biotech company that lasts is to create
patentable material," Woodle says. "If we don't get cash, we'll
have a problem. But if we don't develop patentable technology,
we'll lose our lead."

Pressure for Scientific Shortcuts

With fewer chances to get experiments right, Woodle suggests, Intradigm could come under intense pressure to perform perfectly,
pressure that might lead to sloppy technique and shortcuts. Scientists might not allow enough time to refine lab techniques. They
might look for methods that conserve pricey reagents but don't
produce results that stand up to scrutiny. Or they might go forward
with an experiment even though they're not certain of some initial components of the tests.

"Biotech start-ups are under tremendous pressure to push products they are developing into clinical trials," Victor Li says. "Some-

times these technologies aren't ready for clinical trials, so the FDA decides their trials are a bust, and then that drug or that technology is tainted indefinitely."

Intradigm employees feared that licensing technology to bigger pharmaceutical companies or working with other start-ups might allow their ideas to leak out. Given the company's small size and limited resources, those ideas—closely held, not yet patented, eminently poachable—were its entire ammunition. No other company is as far along in doing this tumor-fighting research with animals, Spears says—a point other industry sources corroborate.

But in licensing technology to large pharmaceutical companies, Intradigm would be helping them develop drugs based on some of Intradigm's discoveries, even as it tries to develop drugs itself. As a result, Intradigm would have to walk a finer, more claustrophobic line, constantly trying to ensure it doesn't give away secrets.

"We would protect ourselves from intellectual-property [IP] theft by keeping the work for big companies in-house, but there are always risks of IP loss," Woodle says. "It's much harder to know what the big pharmaceutical companies are doing than what little biotech competitors are doing—the big firms are quieter, then suddenly they have a patent application in."

Still Hopeful

In February, Woodle and Spears had just returned from a series of meetings with venture capitalists across the country. Like techie Willy Lomans, the founder and the new business head had repeated their pitches, smiled at each investor's questions and jokes, and vowed that their company would outperform other biotechs. They hadn't received any firm commitments of money.

While they were gone, clippings had piled up on Spears's desk: stories from *Science* and the *New York Times* suggesting that, despite the generally poor biotech environment, many larger companies might be tempted to enter Intradigm's field. *Washington Post* articles noted that in 2002 half as many venture-capital firms were active in Washington as two years before and many Washington biotechs were considering shutting down.

Despite the gloomy headlines, the constant travel (economy class, no extra peanuts), and the potential for increased competition, Spears seemed sanguine.

"We still have many venture capitalists left to contact who could lead a second round of financing," he says.

What if none of these leads pan out?

"We'd probably go back to our original funders and ask them to put in more."

And if they decline?

Spears looked away, raised an eyebrow, and let the question hang.

Though Woodle invested more years—and arguably more of his ego and scientific reputation—in the company than anyone else, he appeared relatively upbeat.

"Biotech is a science business," he said. "You hope you combine science and business and don't let one dominate the other. You live with your choices. Ideally, we'd like to get a new round of capital in the range of $10 million to $15 million."

He smiles weakly.

"That's ideal. It's not very realistic, but it's hopeful."

A Gene Therapy Trial Ends in Death and Scandal

By Debra Nelson and Rick Weiss

The promise of dramatic medical breakthroughs has created intense pressure to conduct gene therapy experiments on human volunteers. The standard procedure for bringing a novel therapy to market is to carry out lab research, followed by animal experiments. If these tests are successful, scientists move on to Stage I human trials. If these demonstrate that the therapy is safe, the process continues through second and third stage trials to prove that it is also effective.

In 1999 Jesse Gelsinger, a relatively healthy eighteen-year-old with a rare and usually fatal genetic condition, volunteered for a Stage I gene therapy trial in hopes that others with his condition could be saved. As Debra Nelson and Rick Weiss explain in the following selection, what Gelsinger did not know was that the procedure he had volunteered to undergo had killed two animals in earlier trials and sickened one human subject. Within days of being injected with viruses loaded with corrective genes, Gelsinger fell into a coma and died. After his death, federal regulators and independent researchers criticized the way the trial had been conducted, and the ensuing scandal eventually resulted in lawsuits and the shutdown of the University of Pennyslvania's gene therapy research program. Debra Nelson and Rick Weiss report on health and science for the *Washington Post*.

F our days after scientists infused trillions of genetically engineered viruses into Jesse Gelsinger's liver as part of a novel gene therapy experiment, the 18-year-old lay dying in a hospital bed at the University of Pennsylvania.

His liver had failed, and the teenager's blood was thickening like jelly and clogging key vessels while his kidneys, brain and other organs shut down.

It was a rare and irreversible blood reaction, but it wasn't the first time the researchers had seen it. Unbeknown to Gelsinger, who had signed up for the experimental treatment for a rare and often fatal liver disorder, monkeys that the Penn team had similarly treated had succumbed in very much the same way.

The team had moved forward with the human experiment despite the monkey deaths, and despite criticism from other researchers who thought it was too dangerous, because they believed that a new version of genetically altered virus they had developed was safer than the one that had killed the monkeys.

"Now I have to think, 'Was I blind?'" said James Wilson, head of Penn's Institute for Human Gene Therapy and a lead scientist in the trial. "I'm asking myself that question a lot these days."

First Gene Therapy Casualty

So far, the Penn team's investigation into Gelsinger's death in September [1999]—thought to be the first fatality from gene therapy—has yielded no clear indication of what triggered the fatal reaction, so it's too soon to say whether it should have been predicted and prevented. Besides, experimental therapies by definition often are dangerous, and the distinction between laudable perseverance and unjustifiable risk-taking can be blurry.

Gelsinger's father remains highly supportive of the Penn team. And Gelsinger himself was eager to participate, despite the risks.

But a close look at the Penn research provides a rare snapshot of that subtle scientific and ethical landscape known as the cutting edge of medicine. And it resurrects old questions about whether the Penn experiment ever should have begun.

Many experts wonder, for example, whether an impatient Penn team overlooked the study's pitfalls out of eagerness to win a nine-year-old race to produce the world's first gene-based cure. As scientists work to cure diseases by giving people new, healthy genes, some are asking whether federal regulators' enthusiasm for the hot new field—and their enchantment with Wilson's stellar reputation—may have led them to give Wilson the benefit of the doubt at too many key decision points along the way.

Also anxious for success were the corporate investors who have funneled tens of millions of dollars into a gene therapy company

Wilson founded and into his lab at Penn on the bet that he'd push the field forward.

Wilson adamantly denies that he was influenced by financial concerns. But such tight ties between university researchers and private industry are worrisome to ethicists.

Ethical Shortcomings

A detailed examination of research records, along with interviews with scientists and government officials, has revealed:

• The Penn experiment was the first to shoot such a heavy dose of gene-altered viruses directly into the bloodstream of patients with a genetic disease, even as researchers acknowledged that it had no chance of curing that disease and despite widespread uncertainty in the field about toxic side effects.

• Contrary to most high-risk research, the Penn study experimented with the healthiest rather than sickest segment of the patient population—people such as Gelsinger, who had the disease under control with conventional drugs and diet, or people who had no symptoms at all.

• Researchers were not deterred by early indications of toxicity as they gradually increased doses in their experiment, including an especially severe case of liver damage in one participant. And they discounted or missed evidence of serious side effects in their own and other animal and human studies.

• Volunteers were recruited in ways that federal officials had explicitly precluded as being too potentially coercive, with direct appeals on a patient advocacy Web site that heralded "promising" early results from the clinical trial and said the experiment used "very low doses" when in fact they were relatively high.

• The original consent form, reviewed publicly by the National Institutes of Health, clearly notified prospective participants that monkeys had died from a related treatment, but the final version given to patients eliminated any mention of the deaths.

• Wilson has a financial interest in a private company he founded, Genovo Inc. of Sharon Hill, Pa., which has rights to discoveries made by Wilson at his lab on the Penn campus and which has a substantial financial stake in seeing liver-directed gene therapy succeed. . . .

Gelsinger suffered from a disease called ornithine transcarbamylase (OTC) deficiency. Victims are born with a genetic mutation that leaves their livers unable to break down ammonia, a normal byproduct of metabolism. High ammonia levels can quickly become fatal, and the disease affects newborn boys most seriously, killing about half of them soon after birth.

An estimated 1 in 40,000 babies is born with a defective OTC gene, a tiny population of patients for a major scientific effort. But Wilson, one of the country's leading geneticists, saw an opportunity to tackle a horrific disease while perfecting his technique for delivering genes to the liver, which he considered the key to curing many other more common diseases that have their roots in that organ.

In discussions with colleague Mark Batshaw, who pioneered a drug-and-diet regimen for OTC survivors that has saved numerous lives, Wilson became convinced that OTC deficiency was the perfect disease to prove the potential of gene therapy for the liver. Together, Wilson and Batshaw, with surgeon Steven Raper from Penn, developed a plan to use gene-altered viruses to deliver healthy copies of the OTC gene to affected newborns as soon as they were diagnosed—generally when they were on the brink of death from skyrocketing ammonia levels soon after birth.

The scientists knew the therapy was potentially dangerous, because the gene-altered virus they would use to get the new genes into the newborns' cells can trigger life-threatening reactions. They also knew the therapy would be short-lived, because the babies' immune systems would shut down the new genes within a few days or weeks.

But in such a desperately ill population, for whom no effective treatment exists, the risk of the new therapy would be justified, the researchers reasoned. And once these infants made it through their first crisis, they could be placed on Batshaw's diet-and-drug regimen and perhaps live fairly normal lives.

It seemed like medicine at its best: trying to save babies from an incurable disease. So the team was shocked when Penn's own ethicists rejected the proposal. Parents whose children are so close to death cannot be counted on to make rational decisions about whether to enter those children into a new, potentially dangerous and unproved experiment, they said.

Experimenting on Healthy Subjects

Thus began a change of focus that, in many experts' eyes, triggered an unconscionable shift in the study's balance of risks and benefits: Rather than drop their focus on OTC altogether, the researchers decided to experiment on healthy or stable adult OTC patients such as Gelsinger, who had survived to adulthood because they had milder forms of the disease.

If the treatment proved safe, the researchers could bolster their case for testing its usefulness in newborns. But first they would have to test its safety in adults for whom safe and conventional treatments already existed, whose livers were already stressed because of their disease, and who stood no chance of getting any lasting benefit from the experimental approach.

That shift in focus stirred intense debate in 1995 when the study was reviewed by federal officials. But despite concerns that the researchers still needed to answer some basic scientific questions before moving ahead, the plan—like many other gene therapy protocols then and today—was approved by federal regulators amid a wave of optimism that scientists were on the brink of a breakthrough that would forever change the face of medicine.

"We had to select one disease to move forward in for gene therapy to the liver," Wilson recalled recently. "I thought the severity of the disease would warrant and justify trying this therapy. It's such a compelling story."

Scientists in Business for Themselves?

Wilson also had financial incentives to stay focused on the liver, although he denies that they influenced him in any way.

Since Wilson founded Genovo in 1992, the company has attracted two major corporate investors. While neither of those companies is interested in OTC specifically—it afflicts too few people to be commercially attractive—both are interested in gene delivery to the liver and both were drawn to Genovo's access to Wilson's discoveries.

Biogen Inc. of Cambridge, Mass., has paid Genovo $37 million since 1995 for the right to eventually market various liver- and lung-related genetic therapies developed by Genovo. The deal, which is up for renewal next year [2000], called for Genovo to make progress in moving gene therapy toward a marketable product, said Genovo President Eric Aguiar. Under the agreement, Genovo must share the Biogen money with Wilson's institute at Penn, which today depends on that arrangement for about 20 percent of its budget.

In August [1999], Genovo sealed an additional deal with Genzyme Corp., another biotechnology company in Cambridge, to develop liver-directed gene therapy for metabolic disorders.

Genovo has a direct stake in the genetically engineered adenovirus that Wilson developed for the OTC trial, according to Wilson and Aguiar. If Wilson and his colleagues can demonstrate that the virus is a good vehicle for ferrying genes into the body, the company and Wilson could benefit financially.

In a posting on the Genovo Web site, Aguiar boasts that the relationship with Wilson not only provides the company with access to Wilson's discoveries, but also minimizes business risks, because the company can wait until Wilson's lab tests new treatments on humans before deciding whether to invest in them.

Wilson said he went to great pains to ensure that his business interests would not influence his judgment during the OTC adenovirus trial. Although he was a senior scientist, for example, he gave Raper control over medical and patient care decisions.

Not for the Money

"To suggest that I acted or was influenced by money is really offensive to me," he said. "I don't think about how my doing this work is going to make me rich. It's about leadership and notoriety and accomplishment. Publishing in first-rate journals. That's what turns us on. You've got to be on the cutting edge and take risks if you're going to stay on top."

Nevertheless, Wilson's own financial disclosure statement says Wilson and Genovo "have a financial interest in a successful outcome from the research involved in this study." Wilson acknowledged that the ties with Genovo are tight enough to require him to include that statement on research papers and the consent forms that patients sign when entering his clinical trials, including the OTC experiment.

Academic researchers increasingly are setting up their own companies or business deals on the side. Forty percent of the gene therapy protocols approved in the past three years have had corporate sponsors. Wilson and others argue that sponsorship provides an important source of funding for research and an eventual pipeline to get cures to the public.

Yet the business-academia pipeline has been the subject of much criticism in recent years, because it may sometimes force scientists to choose between good science and good business.

Aguiar said Wilson is too much a scientist to compromise. But Wilson is also very plugged in to the company, Aguiar acknowledged, and calls him on the telephone frequently during the week.

One of those calls from Wilson stands out in both men's memories. It was in September, and the talk was about business. When Aguiar asked how things were going, Wilson said he was having a stressful day. Gelsinger had reacted badly to the treatment and was heading into multiple organ failure in the hospital intensive care unit. "He was really upset about it," Aguiar said.

A Tricky Virus

In their worst-case scenarios, Wilson, Batshaw and Raper thought they might see an inflamed liver in their patients. But the researchers thought they had licked earlier problems with a new, safer brew of genetically engineered adenovirus.

Adenoviruses, a class of viruses that cause the common cold and conjunctivitis, or pinkeye, are extraordinarily efficient at infecting many kinds of human cells. Because of that, they have become popular with gene therapists as a way of delivering helpful genes to sick people. But there are downsides: Adenoviruses trigger intense immune system reactions and can prompt a life-threatening inflammatory response.

Because of those possible problems, many scientists have stopped using adenoviruses to treat genetic diseases and are looking for other, more promising gene delivery systems.

But Wilson's team had worked feverishly during the early 1990s to develop a less inflammatory adenovirus. Over several years, the researchers methodically deleted different combinations of the virus's genes until they had one that seemed to be safe enough to use in the fairly high doses needed to be effective.

The team also spliced copies of the OTC gene into the virus—the payload to be delivered to OTC-deficient patients.

While all four rhesus monkeys that had been given high doses of the first-generation virus had died in previous experiments, subsequent tests of the later viruses on monkeys and mice seemed to confirm that it was less toxic, although it still triggered liver inflammation. By cutting back the dose two hundredfold, the scientists and the FDA [Food and Drug Administration] concluded that they could deliver it safely to humans with no or minimal side effects, especially because humans are so much bigger than monkeys. That is a presumption that federal regulators now question.

But at the time, the Penn researchers were confident in their plan, which included monitoring for early signs of trouble as they gradually increased doses and treating unexpected crises with a proven backup treatment. They commenced treatments in 1997.

Some scientists today remain supportive of Wilson's decision to go forward. "I don't know anyone in gene therapy who has done more animal studies before starting in people," said A. Dusty Miller, a gene therapist at the Fred Hutchinson Cancer Research Center in Seattle.

Calls for Caution

But while the new virus appeared to be safer, there remained wide disagreement over how much safer.

And between the start of the clinical trial and Gelsinger's death in September, new research elsewhere in the field provided further evidence of toxicity and the need for caution in using adenoviruses in the liver.

"Not many people consider it appropriate for treating genetic diseases," said NIH investigator Richard Morgan.

The NIH tested a closely related adenovirus on the livers of three macaque monkeys, which fell seriously ill with symptoms similar to those that killed Gelsinger. They recovered, but one suffered permanent liver damage. A German study involving similar adenoviruses caused acute, toxic responses in rabbits that also resembled those that killed Gelsinger. Cichon, the Berlin researcher who led that study, concluded that adenoviruses should be used only in dire circumstances, such as when the only other alternative is a liver transplant. It is a standard that other scientists say they have adopted.

To give adenoviruses to patients like Gelsinger "would never be justified," Cichon said. "And I am not the only one who thinks this way. We do not understand why [researchers] are taking these risks.". . .

Reluctant Regulators

It hadn't been easy for Wilson and his team to convince federal regulators that they should be allowed to try their approach in people. In 1995, when the researchers first pitched their plan to the NIH committee of scientists and ethicists that then reviewed all gene therapy proposals in advance, several committee members expressed strong reservations. The approach looked too dangerous, they said. And because the immune system would quickly destroy the genetically repaired cells, the treatment would not have any lasting benefit.

But according to several scientists and some NIH committee members, Wilson's charismatic style and his good reputation as a scientist won the day. "Wilson said that you should let people be heroes if they want to be," said Robert Erickson, a committee member at the time and a University of Arizona scientist. "In retrospect, I wish I hadn't been convinced."

The committee approved the protocol but insisted on two changes. The viruses should be infused into a distant blood vessel, not directly into the liver, hopefully reducing the trauma to that already diseased organ. And the researchers should recruit their subjects only through physicians, not by making direct appeals to patients, who might be swayed too easily into participating in the potentially dangerous study.

The researchers agreed, but that's not what happened. First, the FDA became convinced that direct infusion to the liver was preferable and made the team switch back. Penn is now investigating whether that direct infusion contributed to Gelsinger's reaction.

The committee never had a chance to review the change because in 1996, shortly after approving the Penn trial, its powers were greatly reduced by the NIH, under pressure from biotechnology companies seeking relief from federal regulations that the industry deemed overly burdensome.

The NIH committee members say they also never got word of a significant change in the consent form. Although the final form included a perfunctory clause stating that the experiment could result in injury or death, it dropped mention of the original fatal animal studies. Neither the FDA nor the Penn team can explain today why the reference to monkey deaths was dropped.

The Penn team also broke its assurance to the NIH committee that it would recruit participants only through physicians.

In the summer and fall of 1997, Batshaw wrote pieces that appeared in the National Urea Cycle Disorders Foundation newsletter and on its Web site, seeking volunteers. "Obviously, the faster we can complete the Phase I study," he wrote, "the sooner we can move on to the treatment phase in children."

When asked about his call for volunteers, Batshaw said: "We did recruit through the foundation newsletter. It was passive recruitment in that it just appeared there. I wouldn't want to say it was advertised." The possibility of volunteering was merely "posed," he said. As for his comments that some participants had experienced some "correction," he now concedes that might be an overstatement. "Perhaps it could have been stated better."

A Doomed Dream of Helping Babies

There's little question that Gelsinger was a willing and eager participant in the Penn experiment.

He had a mild form of the disease that could be controlled through diet and drugs. He didn't always follow the grueling regimen, and a year ago nearly died from an ammonia attack. But since then, he'd felt better than ever, thanks to a new regimen developed by Batshaw.

After hearing about the experiment from his doctor, he tried to volunteer at age 17—too young for the protocol—then returned as soon as he turned 18. The research team made it clear that the experiment wouldn't cure him, and the teenager also knew there was a small chance it could hurt him. But he was swayed by the scientists' dream that the treatment might someday help severely stricken newborns.

"He wanted to help the babies," said his father, Paul Gelsinger, in a recent interview. "My son had the purest intent."

When Gene Therapy Kills: A Father's Grief

By Paul Gelsinger, interviewed by Stone Phillips

Teenager Jesse Gelsinger died in a 1999 gene therapy experiment gone awry. Jesse had struggled during his childhood with a genetic defect called ornithine transcarbamylase (OTC) deficiency. Although new medications had helped him to control the condition, Jesse volunteered for a gene therapy trial at the University of Pennsylvania's Institute for Human Gene Therapy to help others similarly afflicted. The massive infusion of viruses Jesse received apparently triggered a deadly immune response in the young man.

In the selection that follows, which was taken from a transcript of a *Dateline NBC* television program, Jesse's father, Paul Gelsinger, tells host Stone Phillips that his son had already battled through the worst of the disease before signing up for the study. Immediately after Jesse's death, Paul explains, he felt that physician James Wilson and his team had done all they could ensure the young man's safety. However, others had not been so sure. Prominent gene researcher Robert Erickson explains that while serving on a government review panel four years earlier he had urged rejection of the trial. His concern centered on the severe reactions that some test animals had to the viruses Wilson's team planned to use. Gelsinger says that neither Erickson's concerns nor the animal deaths were mentioned in the risk disclosures before the trial. Gelsinger claims that he was even more shocked when he learned that Wilson had substantial investment in a company that stood to benefit from the trials. Such revelations, he says, eventually led him to file suit against Wilson's team. Gelsinger now serves as vice president of Citizens for Responsible Care and Research (CIRCARE), an organization devoted to protecting human subjects in research and medical treatment. He has testified before Congress and speaks to many groups around the country about his son's experience.

Stone *Phillips:* Good evening. What makes a parent proud? A good report card? A home run in Little League? How about seeing your child hold a door open for a senior citizen with an armful of groceries?

Well, the teen-ager in tonight's story gave his parents a reason to be proud by doing something most of us would consider extraordinary. He volunteered for a medical experiment, one of the 80,000 clinical trials conducted each year in this country. He didn't do it out of desperation; he was not terminally ill. He did it to help doctors find a cure for others. But what happened left his family feeling betrayed by the very doctors they all thought they could trust.

Paul Gelsinger: I saw him to the gate, and I looked him in the eye and told him how proud I was of him, that he was my hero.

Phillips: A proud father of a brave son. Eighteen-year-old Jesse Gelsinger volunteered to help make medical history in an experiment with a world-famous scientist at America's oldest university. But something went terribly wrong. For Paul Gelsinger, a father's fight for answers and accountability would become an agonizing journey through government bureaucracies, to Congress, and finally to court in a case that raises fundamental questions about patients' rights and the honesty and ethics of medical research in America. . . .

Gelsinger: I'm a very slow man to anger. I want to know the truth, and I want to know it all. And I want accountability from everybody. . . .

A Sickly Child

Pattie [Gelsinger, Jesse's biological mother]: Jesse battled for his life his whole life long. And his father has brought him through it every time.

Gelsinger: Jesse went to sleep. And we could not wake him back up.

Phillips: Jesse had lapsed into a coma and doctors at the University of Pennsylvania diagnosed a rare, but serious, genetic problem. An article about him in the *New England Journal of Medi-*

cine explained that because of a defective gene, Jesse had trouble producing one of the enzymes we need to help filter out waste. Without it, dangerous chemicals—like ammonia—could accumulate in his blood and poison his brain, causing confusion, coma, and possibly, even death.

Gelsinger: So this kid had a very rare disorder that was life threatening.

Phillips: In fact, many babies born with the same genetic problem die within weeks. Jesse had survived. But the doctors warned—to stay healthy and keep growing, he would need a special diet and a massive regimen of drugs for the rest of his life.

Gelsinger: It was all based on body weight, and the bigger he got, the more pills he had to take. By the time he was 15, 16, he was up to 54 pills a day. . . .

Mickie [Gelsinger, Jesse's stepmother]: He'd say it's a meal in itself. So, he didn't want eat after that.

Return from a Deep Coma

Phillips: She says simple pleasures like a hamburger were off-limits for Jesse. Eating the wrong foods or skipping his pills could have disastrous consequences. And if there was ever any doubt about that, it was erased in December 1998, mid-way thru Jesse's senior year at this high school in Tucson, Arizona. That Christmas, his family discovered that Jesse, frustrated with the daily mountain of pills, had stopped taking some of his medication.

Gelsinger: I found him on his couch and he looked at me and said, "I can't stop vomiting, and I can't hold anything down. And I'm really scared."

Phillips: They rushed Jesse to the hospital.

Gelsinger: And he started tremors. We had never seen this before.

M. Gelsinger: Oh, we were holding him and he had been shaking. He had been shaking. And then, all of a sudden, one of his breaths, he just stopped.

Gelsinger: This kid wasn't breathing. . . . I thought he had died. For five minutes, I thought my son was dead.

Phillips: But the episode that took him so close to death would lead to a major break-through. Doctors were able to revive Jesse. And switch him to a new, more effective kind of medicine. Almost overnight, his entire life seemed to change.

An Astonishing Improvement

Gelsinger: This kid had never had normal ammonia levels in his life. And now they were the same as you and I.

M. Gelsinger: It was joyous.

Gelsinger: This kid popped out of it. He came out of the coma and wanted to eat. I said: "You want to eat?"

Phillips: And he did start eating?

M. Gelsinger: Oh yes.

Gelsinger: He started eating. This kid put on 40 pounds in four months. . . .

M. Gelsinger: And he was eating anything and everything. And he was enjoying it.

Phillips: He was back on track, and doing as well as ever?

M. Gelsinger: Better.

Gelsinger: Better than ever. . . .

Phillips: Three months after graduating from high school, Jesse Gelsinger had volunteered for a medical experiment that could lead to a revolutionary breakthrough in gene therapy. He knew it wouldn't cure him but it might help save other children who suffered from the same genetic illness he'd been fighting his entire life.

Gelsinger: It's about as pure as it gets. This kid was doing the right thing. . . .

Phillips: But there was something Paul Gelsinger says he didn't know and wasn't told. Years earlier, a scientist just a few miles away from the Gelsinger's home in Tucson [Arizona] had raised serious questions about whether the experiment was safe.

Suppressed Doubts

Robert Erickson: I came in initially quite negative.

Phillips: Dr. Robert Erickson is a prominent gene researcher at the University of Arizona. He had no direct involvement in Jesse's case, but back in 1995, he had been a member of a government panel that reviewed Dr. [James] Wilson's experiment when it was first proposed. In this strongly worded critique, Erickson wrote, "I find this gene therapy protocol unacceptable." Why?

Erickson: An animal dying, or being so sick that it's put down to—to be studied, is obviously a major concern.

Phillips: What troubled Erickson was a report from Dr. Wilson's team that an early version of his genetically-engineered virus had triggered severe reactions, even death, in some animals, apparently because so much of it—trillions of particles—had been injected.

Erickson: Such huge amounts of virus are being given—I mean fantastically more than would ever be produced in our body from an infection, triggering all sorts of inflammatory responses, etc.—have a potential toxicity.

Phillips: Risking that kind of immune system reaction where the body, in effect, turns on itself might be justified, Erickson thought, on terminally ill patients with no other hope. But not on someone like Jesse Gelsinger, whose condition was under control.

The bottom line is, you saw risk with relatively little benefit?

Erickson: That is right, yeah. And I came in very concerned.

Assurances of Safety

Phillips: On the other hand, Erickson says Dr. Wilson's team assured the government reviewers the experiment would be closely monitored for safety. The doses for people would be much lower than the monkeys got, and volunteers would be fully informed of the risks. So despite his reservations, Dr. Erickson ultimately joined others on the government panel in approving the experiment, confident, above all, that it was being supervised by a scientist with an impeccable reputation: Dr. James Wilson. . . . The trouble is, Paul Gelsinger says Dr. Wilson's team had never told him that anyone had ever raised questions about safety.

Gelsinger: No, I had no idea that that had occurred.

Phillips: Nobody ever told you about that?

Gelsinger: No. Nobody had told me about that. . . .

Phillips: There was an autopsy, new tests to make sure the virus—or vector, as it was called—hadn't been contaminated and, two months after Jesse's death, a personal visit from the scientist in charge, Dr. James Wilson.

Gelsinger: He indicated that the vector was everywhere in Jesse's body. They gave this kid 37 trillion viral particles. His body was overwhelmed by it. It was that immune response that killed Jesse. . . .

Phillips: That weekend, a father and the man in charge of the experiment that killed his son, took a late-night hike alone through the Arizona desert for a heart-to-heart talk between two men devastated by the shocking turn of events.

The Doctor Asks for Help

Gelsinger: On our hike out, he was expressing his concern with losing his institute, that, you know, 250 people depended upon his institute remaining open.

Phillips: He was concerned about being shut down?

Gelsinger: That's what he was concerned about. And I turned and I stopped him, and I put my hand on his shoulder, and I looked him in the eye, and I said, "You know Jim, it could be a whole lot worse." I said, "You could lose one of your kids." And that stopped him cold. And he—he stopped and nodded his head and said, "Yeah, you're right."

Phillips: But before the hike ended, Paul Gelsinger says Dr. Wilson made an appeal: for the important work on gene therapy to continue, he needed Paul's support. He asked Paul to fly to east again to meet with his staff and to appear at a government hearing in a public show of support.

Gelsinger: It was vital that my being on their side was a great boost for them, that I would stick in there, and back them up.

Phillips: And you did it?

Gelsinger: And I did it. I was on Penn's side. . . .

Dubious Procedures Uncovered

Phillips: Although Dr. Wilson and his team told scientists, gathered for the meeting, that Jesse's death was unexpected, they also began to acknowledge some irregularities in the way the experiment had been handled. . . .

In addition to those animal deaths Dr. Erickson was concerned about years ago, records revealed others that hadn't been reported. In fact, just a few months before Jesse had signed up for the experiment, several monkeys given viruses similar to Jesse's got sick and two of them died.

The doses were larger, but even so, government rules say reactions like that in animals must be reported in order to protect people. But neither the Gelsingers nor the government was notified.

Gelsinger: They had had adverse reactions in monkeys and they had not reported it to the FDA. In fact, the monkey had the same reaction that Jesse had. . . .

Phillips: And Paul Gelsinger heard something else just as alarming. The rules for the experiment said even if volunteers didn't get visibly ill, if tests showed that any of them had a significant reaction called "grade three," the experiment was supposed to be halted immediately.

Adverse Reactions Ignored

Phillips: Records show there were grade three reactions in more than one patient. The first time, doctors stopped, called the government and got permission to continue, saying an unusual condition with the patient might have been the cause. The second time, they stopped, called and got permission again, citing another unusual condition. But when it happened a third time, they didn't stop, didn't call. And then, a fourth time, they didn't stop or call then, either.

Gelsinger: And they continued anyway, in violation of the protocol. And I had no knowledge of that. . . .

P. Gelsinger: They knowingly went ahead with the whole thing.

Gelsinger: I put them all on notice, that I was going to go seek legal counsel, that too many things had happened here that were not right.

Phillips: Do you believe the doctors at Penn misled you?

Gelsinger: Yes. Absolutely.

Phillips: With so many red flags—from the monkey deaths, to the reactions in other volunteers, even to Jesse's own ammonia levels—why had Dr. Wilson's team allowed the experiment to continue? Now, for the first time, Paul Gelsinger was about to confront a disturbing possibility: that something he never imagined might have played a role in his son's death.

A Financial Incentive

Phillips: Did you know that Dr. Wilson had a big financial stake in a company that had rights to this research? . . .

Gelsinger: This is an outrage, what happened here.

Phillips: Is it wrong for a doctor to want to profit from his research?

Gelsinger: His profit should be attached to his Hippocratic oath. These men take an oath that they're going to take care of their patients, and that their patients are first, and that they will not harm their patients in any way, shape or form. If profits are playing a part in it, are they going to be able to be looking at the patient totally?

Phillips: Even some of James Wilson's fellow gene researchers were surprised at the amount of money involved. One of them, Dr. Robert Erickson, the man who, years earlier, had questioned the safety of the experiment.

Erickson: I did not know the degree of investment that the Institute of Human Gene Therapy at Penn had from private companies. I was quite amazed when I learned that.

Phillips: What did that say to you?

Erickson: Well, it said that institute and many of these other companies are much more tied up with commercial events and probably pressured to have positive results.

Phillips: Certainly at least the appearance of a conflict?

Erickson: Yes. . . .

The Family Sues

Phillips: Alan Milstein is the lawyer the Gelsingers hired to sue one of the world's most honored scientists and one of America's most respected universities. He filed suit even though officials at Penn said everyone in the study, including Jesse, had been adequately warned in lengthy meetings about the risks, and had signed a form saying they understood.

Straight out of the consent form signed by Jesse, quote, "It is even possible that this inflammation could lead to liver toxicity or failure and be life-threatening." I mean, that's pretty black and white, isn't it? Isn't it a pretty clear warning?

[Alan] Milstein: No. There was no information given to Jesse or his family about the monkey deaths. There was no indication given to Jesse or his family about toxic results that—in prior patients. There was no information that would allow Jesse and his family to make any kind of informed decision.

Phillips: Penn says every patient gave informed consent. You were informed and you consented.

Gelsinger: I read that informed consent document. And I read those statements. And they were so down-played and made to appear such a remote possibility that they were not a major consideration in determining whether Jesse should participate in this clinical trial or not.

Phillips: But Paul Gelsinger and his lawyer never had to make that argument in court. Within weeks of filing this lawsuit against the university, Dr. Wilson, and other doctors on his team, the defendants settled without admitting any wrongdoing. Paul Gelsinger agreed not to disclose how much they paid his family, but he refuses to stay silent about what he thinks killed his son. And he says Dr. Wilson and the university aren't the only ones to blame.

Trade Secrets Mask Dangers

Gelsinger: When lives are at stake—and my son's life was at stake —money and fame should take a back seat.

Phillips: He told Congress that other private companies in the race for cures had also been doing gene therapy experiments and had also gotten "adverse reactions." But instead of sharing the information, government rules allowed them to stamp those reactions "confidential," classifying them as trade secrets to protect their research investments. So, while the government knew about them, other researchers like Dr. Wilson and volunteers like Jesse Gelsinger were never allowed to see them.

What did you think when you learned that it was legal to stamp these things "confidential"?

Gelsinger: I was outraged. I had a right to know. Jesse had a right to know. This is probably happening all the time in all kinds of research. And it—it needs to stop. We need to know.

I told this kid he was my hero, and he is. He still is. More so than ever now.

Speaking Out on Safety

Phillips: At public hearings, in private meetings with key lawmakers and in his testimony to Congress, Paul Gelsinger warns there need to be more safeguards and less secrecy to make sure patients are more important than patents.

Gelsinger: The concern should be not on getting to the finish line first, but making sure no unnecessary risks are taken, no lives filled with potential and promise are lost forever, no more fathers lose their sons.

Phillips: Are you opposed now to gene therapy experiments?

Gelsinger: I am not opposed to gene therapy. Do it right. Get it right.

Unreliable Viruses Stall Gene Therapy Research

By Eliot Marshall

The use of fast-acting viruses to insert genes into patients' cells has run into skepticism and regulatory hurdles, science journalist Eliot Marshall reports in the following selection. Just as damaging to gene therapy research, he suggests, are questions about the ethical conduct of some human gene therapy trials. In addition to the death of a healthy volunteer in a University of Pennsylvania gene therapy experiment, Marshall reports that the Food and Drug Administration (FDA) has also alleged misconduct in a gene-based trial for heart disease in Boston. The doubts have led the FDA to suspend several gene therapy trials around the nation. Until the Penn experiment went wrong, researchers had thought that modified adenoviruses would safely and swiftly deliver corrective genes, Marshall says. He notes, however, that critics say there were clear signs that the procedure would be risky. The search for a truly safe viral "vector"—or gene delivery system—has become the FDA's key focus, he reports while scientists in the field are chiefly worried about whether their research can continue. Marshall is senior correspondent for the journal *Science;* he writes primarily on biomedical and bioethical developments.

Dusty Miller, a veteran gene therapy researcher, wants to test a new idea for treating cystic fibrosis. He has engineered a strain of virus to create a new "vector" to inject useful genes into cells. He has tested it in his lab at the Fred Hutchinson Cancer Research Center in Seattle, getting "wonderful" results in mice. Although he can't guarantee that it's safe for human use,

Eliot Marshall, "Gene Therapy on Trial," *Science*, vol. 288, May 12, 2000, pp. 951–57. Copyright © 2000 by the American Association for the Advancement of Science. Reproduced by permission.

he's confident that it is. Yet he's hesitating about testing it in patients, stretching out preliminary research while using an established but, he thinks, less efficient vector in volunteers. He's being supercautious, he says, because the "climate for gene therapy"
has turned cold.

The chill set in on 17 September 1999. That's when Jesse
Gelsinger, a young volunteer, died in a gene therapy trial at the
University of Pennsylvania in Philadelphia, triggering a blitz of
media and government attention. The Food and Drug Administration (FDA) has issued Penn a warning letter and shut down all
clinical trials at Penn's Institute for Human Gene Therapy while
it investigates what happened.

Another Study Halted

The chill intensified last week [early May 2000] when FDA made
public a warning letter to cardiac specialist Jeffrey Isner of St. Elizabeth's Medical Center in Boston, alleging infractions of FDA rules
in a gene therapy trial for heart disease in which one patient's cancer could have been exacerbated by the treatment and, FDA contends, a death was not properly reported. Isner's studies are now
on hold. FDA also halted several other gene therapy trials around
the country last winter while investigating vector toxicity.

Public attention in this round of reports and investigations is
likely to focus on who's to blame for errors, whether patients were
adequately informed of the risks, and whether the tangle of relationships among companies, investigators, and institutions has created unacceptable conflicts of interest in the field. Many clinicians
fear that support for gene therapy will buckle under the onslaught.
At the scientific level, what happened at Penn holds two important lessons that are likely to get swamped in the publicity.

The first is the story of the vector James Wilson, director of
Penn's gene therapy institute, and his team used: a patented version of a common respiratory tract virus—adenovirus—that had
been stripped of certain genes to make it more innocuous. Researchers had once pinned their hopes on adenovirus vectors, be-
lieving they would overcome a basic problem that has dogged gene
therapy since its inception: the difficulty of getting genes into target cells and, once there, getting the genes to express their proteins.

Now some investigators think that, because of their inherent problems, adenovirus vectors may be limited to narrow uses. The prob-

lem is, every vector that has been investigated also has limitations. The adenovirus capsid protein, which encases the genome, may trigger a powerful immune reaction at high doses, many researchers believe. It is essential for transporting genes into target cells.

The second lesson involves the nature of clinical research itself. Although it's a shock when a patient dies in a toxicity test, says a clinician who has supervised many such trials, it is not unusual.

"If you were to look in [a big company's] files for testing small-molecule drugs," he insists, "you'd find hundreds of deaths." Often, warning signs become clear only in retrospect, and many clinicians believe that's what happened in the Penn trial. Hints of toxicity had cropped up in previous experiments done by Wilson and others, but the Penn team may have been misled in one crucial respect by animal data that did not translate to humans.

But others suggest that clinicians at Penn should have been more sensitive to the risks, especially because they were injecting a potentially toxic vector into relatively healthy volunteers.

"There were many places where this should have been stopped," says Huntington Willard, a molecular geneticist at Case Western Reserve University in Cleveland and a member of the American Society of Human Genetics board. Several leaders in the field have said that they knew that directly injecting the livers of volunteers with huge quantities of immunogenic viral particles (38 trillion at the highest dose) was risky. But they did not intervene, and the trial was given a green light by several local and federal agencies.

Today, Willard sees "a very strong parallel" between a rush to the clinic in gene therapy and the space shuttle Challenger explosion. "It takes an event like that," he says, to let people see "just how dangerous some of this stuff really was." Willard concludes that "we need to take a much more sober view of where this field is going."

Design by Committee

Regardless of what the critics think, says Arthur Caplan, director of Penn's Institute for Bioethics, people designed this gene therapy trial with the best intentions. He recalls how Mark Batshaw, a pediatrician at Penn in the early 1990s, now at Children's National Medical Center in Washington, D.C., wanted to save children born with a deadly liver problem. The disease occurs when a gene on the X chromosome is missing or defective, producing too little of a liver enzyme, ornithine transcarbamylase (OTC), that's needed to remove ammonia from the blood. Many infants become comatose at birth and die.

Some with mild deficiencies—like Jesse Gelsinger—can survive if they keep to a strict diet and take compounds that help eliminate ammonia. But there's no substitute for natural OTC. And even mild deficiencies can be deadly. Gelsinger, for example, neglected his OTC regimen and nearly died in 1998. Caplan says Batshaw "was the pivotal guy" in Penn's OTC gene research:

"He was tired of burying babies."

Batshaw, Wilson, and a surgeon at Penn named Steven Raper, the principal investigator, devised a plan in 1994–95 to transfer healthy OTC genes into people who lack them. (Through a Penn spokesperson, Raper and Wilson declined to comment.) The objective, according to the protocol, was to develop "a safe recombinant adenovirus" that could infect the livers of patients and release OTC. Wilson's institute at Penn and the private company he founded had additional goals: to develop vectors for treating liver diseases and other illnesses.

The improved adenovirus vector developed at Penn seemed like a "wonder vector" back in 1995, Miller recalls. It was easy to grow, versatile, capable of infecting both dividing and nondividing cells, targeted the liver (as everyone assumed), and was quick to express genes in tissue. This vector was the right tool, Batshaw still argues: "Adenovirus is the only one that works rapidly enough, even now."

He explains that whereas most other vectors take 3 to 6 weeks to begin working, adenovirus vector starts to express genes within 24 hours. This could be crucial for treating newborns with severe cases of the disease. You need quick action, he says, "if you're trying to get kids out of hyperammonemic coma" and prevent death or mental retardation. "Our plan was to use the adenovirus to get them out of coma; that would last for a few months," then go to second-stage gene therapy with a different vector—one problem with this vector is that gene expression is of limited duration—or possibly to liver transplantation.

But the plan changed when ethicists looked at it. Caplan, who was recruited to Penn shortly after Wilson, argued that it would be preferable to begin with adult volunteers because the trial was designed only to test toxicity. Later, infants could be enrolled. The initial subjects would have no chance of benefiting, in part because adenovirus vector can be given only once. It sets up an immune response that usually causes the body to eliminate the vector if it is used again. This meant that no one who took part in this trial could hope to benefit from adenovirus gene therapy at a later time.

Even in ordinary circumstances, Caplan says, obtaining parental consent for experiments on children is "a problem." But it's especially tough "if you're trying to explain to parents in the middle of a crisis that you're only doing a safety study" that would not help a critically ill child. Caplan argued that it was "wrong to do nontherapeutic research on someone who cannot consent."

Searching for the Right Vector

Researchers have been trying for more than a decade to create a tamer adenovirus. The virus is shaped like an icosohedral box studded with "penton" bases that support long fibers—described by FDA gene therapy specialist Philip Noguchi as "a cannonball with spikes." The box, or capsid, shields the genome. Modifications such as those used by Wilson and Crystal have focused on editing out key bits of DNA inside the capsid that are expressed early during infection of a cell, genes labeled E1 through E4, which trigger immune reactions.

The goal is to make the vector as stealthy as possible. The fewer viral proteins the immune system "sees," the less likely it will attack. And the longer the vector survives, the better its chances of delivering therapeutic genes.

For the OTC trial, Wilson used a version with E1 and E4 genes deleted. In his cystic fibrosis trials, Crystal has used a version with E1 and E3 deleted, which he claims can even be given safely in repeat doses. Since switching to an inhaled spray containing this new vector, Crystal says, "we have had no significant serious toxicities."

Some scientists have also attempted to create fully "gutless" vectors by hollowing out all viral genes and replacing them with substitutes. They include Jeffrey Chamberlain at the University of Michigan, Ann Arbor, Beaudet and Larry Chan at Baylor, and a group at Merck in Whitehouse Station, New Jersey, under former executive Thomas Caskey. Beaudet and Caskey say researchers in their labs have observed virtually no toxicity when their gutless vector is given to mice at high doses. However, it is hard to eliminate contamination by live "helper" virus and to produce high-concentration batches. High doses may still be required to produce a clinical benefit, and, as Boucher suggested in 1995, high doses may run into toxicity from capsid proteins. Wilson suggested as much in [a] RAC meeting, and Noguchi and FDA toxicologist Anne Pilaro have raised this possibility in several meetings. So has Salk's Verma, who co-authored a 1998 study of adenovirus vector that called for a "reevaluation" of its use in long-term gene therapy.

Recently, FDA staffers heard from another scientist who concluded 5 years ago that adenovirus capsid protein toxicity was a problem: Prem Seth, senior scientist at the Human Gene Therapy Research Institute in Des Moines, Iowa. Based on studies he did in the mid-1990s, he concluded that "empty capsids appear to be immunogenic, like intact virus," and produce similar effects, like cytokine release. He never published the data, because "there wasn't much interest."

This analysis suggests that even gutless vectors may be dangerous in some circumstances, but the jury is not in. "It's still debatable," says Chamberlain. Beaudet agrees: "Based on our published mouse data," he says, "we think the capsid proteins are not a big problem." But he concedes that there are "not convincing data yet" from nonhuman primates to settle the issue.

As far as Noguchi is concerned, "the most critical issue for the field right now" is determining the risk of these new, "safe" vectors. "Are there two types of toxicity with adenovirus or just one?" he asks. Is the shell itself a problem, in addition to viral gene expression? "What is its inherent toxicity? Is this the dose-limiting thing? We need to rethink these hard questions."

For many people in the field, however, the critical question over the next few months is whether they will be able to continue gene therapy trials while everyone rethinks these questions.

Improving the Safety of Gene Therapy Trials

By Jay P. Siegel

As Jay P. Siegel explains in the following selection, originally presented as testimony before the U.S. Senate's Subcommittee on Public Health on February 2, 2000, the federal government oversees all experiments involving human subjects. It requires each research institution to ensure ethical conduct, obtain informed consent from each participant, and balance the risk associated with clinical trials against the potential benefits. Responsibility for overseeing gene therapy research falls on the Center for Biologics Evaluation and Research (CBER), a part of the Food and Drug Administration (FDA). As Siegel notes, serious questions about events that caused the 1999 death of volunteer Jesse Gelsinger in a gene therapy experiment at the University of Pennsylvania led Congress to hold hearings on whether the safety of gene therapy trials was being monitored effectively. Siegel tries to put some of these fears to rest by explaining that researchers are required to report any negative results during animal studies. He also claims that the FDA may respond to initial trials by requiring a modification of experiments, a change in eligibility, or even a suspension of the trial. He also outlines further steps the FDA is taking in the aftermath of the Gelsinger case to assure the safety of gene therapy trials. Siegel is director of CBER's Office of Therapeutics Research and Review.

ood morning, Mr. Chairman and Members of the Committee. Thank you for Inviting the Food and Drug Administration (FDA or the Agency) to participate in this

Jay P. Siegel, testimony before the U.S. Senate Committee on Health, Education, Labor and Pensions, Subcommittee on Public Health, Washington, DC, February 2, 2000.

hearing concerning gene therapy and the Federal government's role in the oversight of this field of medical research. I am Dr. Jay P. Siegel, Director, Office of Therapeutics Research and Review, Center for Biologics Evaluation and Research (CBER), Food and Drug Administration. The Office of Therapeutics Research and Review is the office within FDA responsible for the regulation of gene therapy.

Before I begin, I would like to express, on behalf of the Administration, our continued concern that gene therapy studies be as safe as possible. As you know, when we recently discovered potential safety violations with clinical trials being conducted at the Institute for Human Gene Therapy located at the University of Pennsylvania we took rapid and appropriate action. We will continue to investigate this situation thoroughly and take appropriate action to help protect patients participating in gene therapy clinical trials throughout the country. . . .

The Growing Scope of Therapies

Gene therapy has the potential to revolutionize the treatment of diseases that currently are incurable or have inadequate treatments. Cell and gene therapy products constitute an emerging area of therapeutic intervention that has only existed for just over a decade. The relative newness and complexity of the science of gene therapy presents considerable challenges in accomplishing product regulation. Whereas many biotechnology products consist of single purified proteins and antibodies, these novel therapies combine cells, tissues and even organs with genetic alterations, novel device delivery systems and use of specialized growth factors.

The original rationale for gene therapy was to treat genetic diseases by replacing a nonfunctional or defective gene. An example of such a disease for which gene therapy shows promise involves a genetic error that causes an individual to lack an enzyme which leads to a condition where the patient cannot mount an immune response to common infections. This disease, severe combined immunodeficiency, is extremely rare and has been also called the "bubble baby syndrome."

Currently, gene therapy studies are examining a broad range of potential therapeutic interventions, including stimulating the body's immune reaction to tumors, inducing new blood vessels in the heart to alleviate heart attacks, and stopping the replication of HIV in AIDS patients. There is also renewed emphasis on gene therapies for genetic diseases such as hemophilia A and B, and cystic fibrosis.

Since the first human gene transfer in the late 1980's, human gene therapy products have become one of the fastest growing areas of product development under FDA oversight. In 1993, the Agency published a Federal Register notice which provided clarification that cell and gene therapies were subject to regulation under the Public Health Service (PHS) Act and the Federal Food, Drug, and Cosmetic (FD&C) Act. Gene therapy products present extraordinarily novel and controversial issues associated with cutting edge medical technology, ranging from the use of mouse and human viruses to produce gene vectors (carriers of genes), to the ethical and social issues involved with the potential for gene alteration in utero and other uses which could affect future generations.

In the five-year period from 1989 to 1993, 48 gene therapy investigational new drug applications (INDs) were submitted to FDA. In contrast, from the publication of the 1993 Federal Register notice until January 19, 2000, 240 gene therapy INDs were submitted to FDA. Of those, 55 were submitted in the most recent Fiscal Year (FY) 1999. There have also been over 800 amendments (e.g., changes to the product, or new protocols, etc.) to gene therapy INDs submitted each year. The Agency has yet to receive the first application to license a gene therapy product.

Regulation of Human Testing

For any unproved biological product that is to be tested in humans, an IND must be filed with FDA. The IND process for gene therapy is the same as it is for other biologic products. We encourage and recommend meetings between CBER reviewers and sponsors of a potential IND for all biological products throughout the product development process in order to stimulate scientific interchange and clarify FDA regulatory requirements. Under statutory authority, FDA determines within 30 calendar days from receipt of an IND whether it is appropriate for the IND to proceed or, if necessary, to place an IND on clinical hold, in order to protect the safety of human subjects. This is a difficult task for novel therapies with relatively unknown risks.

Part of the FDA's review of the IND includes a review of the sponsor's proposed or FDA's recommended stopping rules. The stopping rules are rules in the protocol which assure that a clinical trial will be stopped if certain adverse events should occur. In addition, prior to allowing a clinical protocol to proceed under an IND, FDA frequently requires several modifications to the protocol to ensure that all known safety issues have been addressed. These might include: changes in manufacturing to ensure purity, additional laboratory testing of the product, additional animal testing of a product, exclusion of human subjects who might be at high risk for serious adverse events, additional safety testing of human subjects, lower starting doses in humans and slower escalation of doses. These modifications to the protocol are intended to lower the risk to human subjects.

As clinical data accumulate and product development continues, FDA continues to monitor the IND and may require further changes, for example, when adverse events are reported. On occasion, or when information raises concerns regarding the quality of the investigational product or conduct of the clinical trial, the Agency may perform an inspection.

In addition, CBER conducts regulatory research, as needed, to assist in the assessment of product safety. An example of such regulatory research is the development of assays to detect the presence of replication competent mouse retrovirus. The development of these assays are intended to help assure the safety and quality of mouse retroviral vectors used in gene therapies and therefore lead to marketing of safe products by many firms.

Institutional Review Board

As with all IND studies, an Institutional Review Board (IRB) must review and approve such studies in advance to ensure the rights and welfare of study participants. The IRB plays a critical role in the review process, particularly in determining the continuing adequacy of protocols and with regard to its approval of informed consent forms which explain the known and potential risks and benefits to human subjects.

Although no product is risk-free, FDA's goal is to minimize the risks by assessing information on the product and conduct of the clinical trial including the safety reports it receives from the sponsors of the investigational therapy and similar therapies. It should be stressed that it is the sponsors and investigators of clinical trials who conduct the clinical trials and, therefore, they have primary responsibility to protect the safety of the patients or individuals participating in the trials. FDA helps assure that sponsors/investigators are meeting their obligations through the IND review process. . . .

Reporting of Adverse Events

Once the clinical trial has begun, the sponsors and clinical investigators have regulatory responsibilities with respect to reporting adverse events associated with gene therapy products. These requirements, which are the same as those for any new IND, specify that any adverse event associated with the use of the study drug that is both serious and unexpected must be reported to FDA as soon as possible, and no later than fifteen calendar days of the sponsor receiving the information. Any findings for tests in laboratory animals that suggest a significant risk for the human subjects must be reported by the sponsor within the same time frame. Additionally, an unexpected fatal or life threatening experience associated with the use of the drug must be reported as soon as possible by the sponsor but no later than 7 calendar days after the sponsor receives the information. All other adverse events must be reported in an annual report.

The information provided in the adverse event reports is reviewed by FDA to determine whether additional actions are warranted to assure the safety of the study participants. Actions that might be taken by FDA, sponsor, investigator, or IRB could include:

• notifying sponsors with INDs for related or identical products about safety concerns;

• modifying the protocol to include changes in eligibility criteria, changes in dose, route, and schedule of administration of the product;

• changing the informed consent to disclose new toxicity;

• obtaining additional consent from current study participants to reflect new information;

• updating the clinical investigator's brochure;

• considering the need for new non-clinical studies; and,

• placing the IND(s) on clinical hold.

When an ongoing study is placed on clinical hold, no new subjects may be recruited to the study and treated with the investigational therapy; patients already in the study are taken off the investigational therapy unless specifically permitted to continue by FDA, based on the particular circumstances of each study.

The Jesse Gelsinger Case

One of the issues that this Subcommittee has asked us to address is the case involving the death of a young patient in a gene therapy clinical trial at University of Pennsylvania. As the Subcommittee knows, this involves an ongoing investigation. In order to ensure that this investigation is thorough and effective, we are limited in the discussion we can have today regarding findings that are, necessarily, preliminary. FDA investigators have concluded an inspection at the University of Pennsylvania. Based upon the FDA investigators' findings, a notice of inspection observations (FDA Form 483) was issued to Dr. James Wilson on January 19, 2000, as is often done at the conclusion of an FDA inspection. The items listed on the FDA Form 483 represent the investigators' observations concerning potential deficiencies relating to the clinical investigation. In this case, the investigators' observations listed on the FDA Form 483 pertain to some of the following issues: informed consent; implementing patient exclusion criteria; following stopping rules; initiating protocol changes; and, submitting reports of animal deaths. Based upon the concerns raised regarding the adequacy of the monitoring program to protect the safety of human subjects, FDA determined it would be prudent to place all other trials sponsored by Dr. James Wilson and the Institute for Human Gene Therapy on clinical hold pending demonstration that an adequate monitoring program is in place. FDA will further evaluate the inspection findings and the sponsor's response to determine the significance of the observations and if regulatory or additional administrative action is necessary to achieve corrections. FDA will consider the full range of options and, if necessary, take further Agency action.

At the December RAC meeting, FDA provided a complete presentation concerning our adverse event reporting requirements, definitions and procedures. This presentation, along with FDA presentations delivered at other forums, should help sponsors and investigators better understand FDA's requirements with regards to adverse event reporting. FDA's ex-officio non-voting representative was present at this meeting. FDA staff also delivered several presentations on the use of adenoviral vectors and the clinical trial at the University of Pennsylvania. The use of adenoviral vectors was extensively discussed at the December RAC meeting. At the next RAC meeting in March 2000, the ad-hoc working group will present and issue a report on the adverse events reported by investigators using adenoviral vectors. This ad-hoc RAC working group, including representatives of FDA and NIH, is working together to evaluate the relationship between adenovirus vectors and the adverse events. FDA hopes this effort may result in the improvement of human subject safety through the identification of clinical trials that may need additional monitoring.

In order to protect human subjects and also increase public knowledge of adverse events, FDA and NIH have taken steps to remind sponsors of their reporting requirements. In the letter dated November 5, 1999, FDA also included information to the clinical investigators and sponsors reminding them of their responsibilities to report adverse events. . . .

Meeting a Growing Caseload

With the number of gene therapy IND submissions increasing each year, FDA has continually evaluated its review and oversight processes, to ensure better human subject protection, to improve investigator compliance, to improve the quality of submitted protocols, and to provide additional guidance and standards to facilitate preparation of INDs. This has been done through educational outreach, conferences, meetings and policy development.

CBER staff serve as faculty for a number of educational programs for sponsors and investigators of INDs. Each year CBER gives numerous presentations on scientific and regulatory issues and policy as they relate to gene therapy and other biological product investigations.

FDA has sponsored or co-sponsored many educational outreach programs, including co-sponsoring three open public Gene Therapy Policy Conferences with NIH that discussed scientific and ethical issues, such as vector safety, and ethical considerations regarding prenatal gene therapies, and Gene Therapy Workshops with over 800 people attending each workshop. During these conferences and workshops, FDA presented information to sponsors and investigators on FDA requirements, recommendations and policies for gene therapy INDs. FDA held educational symposia at the 1998 and 1999 annual meetings of the American Society for

Gene Therapy (ASGT) and will expand its symposia at the ASGT annual meeting in 2000. FDA continues to work with ASGT toward the development of standard approaches to preclinical toxicology studies and facilities standardization.

FDA also partners with many patient groups to provide regulatory and scientific support at patient group meetings. Such efforts with the Cystic Fibrosis Foundation and with the National Hemophilia Foundation have contributed to the initiation of a number of gene therapy trials for those diseases.

FDA reviews annual reports, which include data on patient accrual, adverse events, and scientific and medical reports. The Office for Protection from Research Risks (OPRR) and FDA educate the research community on issues related to protecting human research subjects. Both respond to questions from researchers, IRBs and institutional officials. FDA and OPRR co-sponsor several workshops annually for the research community.

Plans for the Future

FDA strives to evaluate and implement measures to improve the conduct of clinical studies. In addition to the actions mentioned previously, CBER intends to take the following steps to improve human subject safety:

• Plan to issue a proposed rule on the public disclosure of information regarding clinical trials of gene therapies that would provide more information on gene therapy clinical trials to the public.

• Continue efforts to improve investigator compliance through educational outreach for sponsors and investigators.

• Enhance regulatory research to improve product safety.

• Provide additional guidance for gene therapy products to build upon existing guidance. In this last regard, CBER issued two guidance documents, "Guidance for Industry: Guidance for Human Somatic Cell Therapy and Gene Therapy" and "Draft Guidance for Industry: Supplemental Guidance on Testing for Replication Competent Retrovirus in Retroviral Vector Based Gene Therapy Products and During Follow-up of Patients in Clinical Trials Using Retroviral Vectors."

• Conduct more inspections to increase oversight of gene therapy INDs.

• Encourage sponsors to assess or reassess the adequacy of their monitoring program and to consider obtaining independent monitoring as needed to improve the conduct of their trials and help ensure timely and accurate reporting to oversight bodies.

Responsibility for Safety

In the area of gene therapy, it is clear that many exciting innovations are emerging. While many of these new gene therapy and biotech products may yet have unknown risks, they also have the potential for tremendous patient benefit. When developing these new products, sponsors of clinical trials must accept responsibility to ensure that participants are not exposed to known unreasonable risks and that the experimental products are as safe as possible. I have outlined FDA's role in this process and have briefly mentioned our interactions with NIH. It is critically important that sponsors and investigators who conduct the clinical trials take the responsibility to assure the safety of their human subject participants. They must achieve this by using quality controlled experimental products, by practicing good clinical medicine and also by communicating accurate information to FDA regarding safety in a timely manner, as required by our regulations.

CBER is committed to minimizing the risks to human subjects who participate in clinical trials, including gene therapy studies, while encouraging the development of promising new experimental therapies. We will continue to work closely with NIH and others as appropriate. It is essential that FDA continue to develop the strongest possible science base so that our reviewers possess the necessary scientific and medical knowledge to effectively review and evaluate new and increasingly complex investigational biological products such as gene therapy.

We know that these issues present new and difficult challenges. I believe we have met these challenges in the past and let me assure the Committee that we will continue to do so in the future.

Some Gene Therapy Trials Resume While Others Remain Frozen

By Raja Mishra

Gene therapy's greatest success took a tragic turn in 2002 when cancer arose in two of the young patients who received treatment to correct their lack of an immune system. The development prompted the federal government to halt gene therapy trials on human subjects in December 2002. In the following selection Raja Mishra reports that months later, a panel of regulators at the Food and Drug Administration (FDA) voted to allow twenty-seven of more than two hundred gene therapy trials to go forward. However, in light of concerns that gene therapy's one clear success—the treatment of children born without a functioning immune system—apparently caused leukemia, the FDA panel now insists on proof that volunteers for the experimental treatments understand the risks, Mishra reports. Despite the FDA's action, many other gene therapy trials remain stalled. One member of the panel objected to the FDA's action in allowing the twenty-seven trials to proceed, saying that researchers should first understand how gene therapy can lead to cancer in some patients. Mishra, a reporter for the *Boston Globe*, frequently reports on health issues.

Restoring momentum to a beleaguered experimental medical field, federal officials yesterday [on February 28, 2003] permitted 27 recently halted gene therapy patient trials to proceed despite revelations that the advanced technique caused cancer in two young patients.

Federal officials froze the trials last December [2002] after French researchers reported the cancer cases, raising fears among some researchers that gene therapy would remain under an ethical cloud for years. The much-touted field, in which doctors attempt to cure patients by inserting genes into them, is still recovering from the 1999 death of a test patient.

The suspended trials were a small but marquee group among the more than 200 US gene therapy patient experiments underway, cleverly using a common virus to deliver genes inside cells that could potentially treat cancer, HIV [the virus that causes AIDS], multiple sclerosis, immune disorders, and other ailments. The use of the virus had actually worked well in treating so-called "bubble boy syndrome," but the cancer cases made clear that the virus can do damage as well.

Mandatory Cancer Warnings

But yesterday, a research panel convened by the Food and Drug Administration agreed the technique's healing potential outweighed the cancer risk. They voted, with only one "nay" among 21 members, to green-light the suspended trials. The endorsement, however, came with a caveat: Each gene therapy researcher involved in those trials must convince federal officials that all patients undergoing the experimental treatments are amply warned of its cancer risks.

The FDA will "now go back and look at each trial in an active mode," said Dr. Philip D. Noguchi, the FDA's chief gene therapy regulator. "We'll work with each researcher through all the issues."

Patient safety advocate Paul Gelsinger, whose teenage son Jesse's death in a 1999 gene therapy experiment prompted a federal overhaul of the research, approved of the panel's decision, particularly praising its openness, a contrast with the initial secrecy surrounding his son's death.

The panel refused to give the go-ahead to two recently suspended US trials similar to the French research that gave the two boys cancer. They involve X-linked severe combined immune deficiency disease or X-SCID, commonly known as "bubble boy" disease after a 1980s high-profile case in which a patient lived within a sealed plastic enclosure to guard against infection.

The FDA will review each patient involved in these two trials to determine whether they possess a heightened risk of developing cancer, and if all means of conventional treatment have been exhausted. A third related trial, involving a variation of SCID, will also be restricted in the same way.

The two French cancer cases arose in X-SCID patients, who were born without a critical immune system gene, making them extremely vulnerable to viruses. Even the common cold can be a mortal threat, and many must live in sealed sterile rooms. Most die during childhood. A matched bone marrow transplant can help, though these risky and rare procedures often fail.

Gene therapy scored its first—and only—success to date against this daunting condition.

Researchers at the Necker Hospital in Paris removed the faulty immune cells from patients, all infants. The cells were mixed in a lab dish with a retrovirus, a type of virus that wedges its own DNA directly into a patient's DNA. But this was no ordinary retrovirus: researchers stripped it of dangerous genes, then inserted the very immune system gene the patients lacked. In the lab dish, the retrovirus did its job, infecting the bone marrow cells. The modified bone marrow cells were then put back in patients.

It worked, generating headlines around the world. The bone marrow spread the corrective gene, quickly rebuilding the infants' immune systems. Nine of 11 patients responded, and were soon discharged from the hospital to live, for the first time in their lives, like normal children.

The success, in 2001, electrified the field, which was still reeling from Jesse Gelsinger's death.

Uncontrolled Cell Growth

But troubling news arrived last September [2002]. One boy developed leukemia, a blood cancer. Analysis indicated the retrovirus had wedged itself on top of a gene called LMO2, involved in cell replication. The disturbed LMO2 gene caused the bone marrow cells to multiply uncontrollably—and a patient that once desperately needed healthy immune cells had too many, causing cancer.

The boy was put on high-dose chemotherapy. But researchers

figured the cancer was a fluke. But in December came a second leukemia case, prompting the FDA to suspend all gene therapy trials that use a retrovirus to deliver treatment.

The two children with leukemia are "doing well," said Dr. Marina Cavazzana-Calvo of Necker University. The other seven patients responding to the treatment continue to live normal lives.

The FDA panel, comprised of researchers, ethicists, and patient advocates, unanimously agreed that bubble boy patients should only get gene therapy if all other treatment options were exhausted. Before, some researchers viewed gene therapy as equivalent to the conventional treatment, bone marrow transplantation, rather than last ditch.

"It's not easy striking the right balance here," said panel member and ethicist Thomas Murray of the Hastings Center in New York. Murray supported lifting the suspension of the 27 gene therapy trials. The lone dissenter on that vote was John Coffin of Tufts University, who said that researchers still know little about the biology behind the cancerous side effects, and approvingly cited the cautious approach of another high-profile scientific probe.

"We're not going to send space shuttles up until we find out what happened to the Columbia," he said.

A Heart Treatment Revives Hopes for Gene Therapy

By Marilynn Marchione

In the selection that follows, Marilynn Marchione reports that after numerous disappointments, gene therapy has begun to prove successful in helping to save some people's lives. As an example, Marchione presents the case of Ruth Bettin, a woman whose heart was giving out because the arteries that supply it with blood were clogged. After all conventional treatments failed, she received an experimental therapy in 1999 in which genes were injected into her heart to promote the growth of new blood vessels. Although she is not cured, Marchione reports, the therapy has apparently helped Bettin survive years longer than expected and live a more normal life. This success stands out against many gene therapy setbacks, she notes, including failure to cure cystic fibrosis and several patient deaths. These setbacks led to suspension of some gene therapy trials and resulted in a reduction of interest in the field. However, new strategies for gene delivery and a more modest set of goals are bringing about a revival of optimism in the field, she reports. Marilynn Marchione is a health columnist for the *Milwaukee Journal Sentinel*.

R uth Bettin was only 9 years old when scientists cracked the genetic code [by discovering the structure of DNA]. Fifty years later, she's probably alive because of it.

Bettin endured two heart bypass surgeries, three balloon angioplasties and five stent procedures to open blocked arteries, only to have them reclog within weeks. Doctors listed her for a heart transplant but said she might not survive the wait for the operation. Conventional medicine could offer her no more.

"They were just out of options," the Beloit, Wis., woman said. "I was so unstable they just did not hold out a lot of hope."

Her cardiologist, the University of Wisconsin-Madison's Matthew Wolff, called around the country, searching for something new to try.

He found Jeffrey Isner, a Boston doctor pioneering a radical treatment: injecting patients' hearts with a gene that promotes the growth of blood vessels. It was so risky that some people died from the procedure itself.

"It's really designed for desperate patients, and Ruth was a desperate patient," Wolff said.

Not a Cure but a Lifesaver

Bettin had the treatment in January 1999. Four years later, she is not cured, but is alive against all odds, taking fewer medications and trying to build up time on the treadmill at the gym.

"Walking and breathing was difficult before," she said. "A couple years ago, we had the river festival in Beloit, and my kids pushed me around in a wheelchair because there was no way I could walk the distance of the park. The last couple years I've taken grandchildren, and I go on rides with them. We go on the Tilt-A-Whirl and all those things."

She is among a small but growing number of people for whom gene therapy is finally starting to pay off after a decade of stunning failures—a teenager dying in one experiment and two toddlers developing a cancer-like disease in another.

"Gene therapy has taken a lot of knocks," said George Daley, a scientist at one of the nation's leading genetics centers, the Whitehead Institute in Cambridge, Mass. "The early stuff was a nightmare. It was worthless."

But many scientists think that gene therapy now has been redirected in ways that may finally make it more safe and successful, though that may wind up being for a much smaller set of diseases and problems than originally hoped.

Thousands of people in the United States are currently [in 2003] enrolled in about 200 gene therapy experiments, more than half of them for cancer. All are clinical trials regulated by the Food and Drug Administration.

Several times, federal officials have halted many of these trials, worried about unforeseen consequences from a technology so new that predicting every possible outcome is virtually impossible.

After each interruption and review by overseers, most of the trials have resumed because the reality is that gene therapy remains many people's only hope of defeating fatal diseases.

"The concept is very simple," said Nelson Wivel, a University of Pennsylvania scientist who for many years headed the National Institutes of Health office responsible for overseeing gene therapy experiments in the United States.

The idea is to give people the correct or healthy version of a gene they lack. People with Parkinson's disease, for instance, would get a gene that directs production of the brain chemical dopamine. Diabetics would get genes for insulin. Cancer patients would get tumor suppressor genes to put the brakes on rampant cell growth.

It all seemed doable in 1990, in the first U.S. gene therapy experiment on a 4-year-old girl with a severe immune system disorder caused by a defect in one of her genes.

About 2,800 diseases or disorders are believed to be caused by single gene defects. It was these "easy targets" that researchers first set their sights on trying to cure. A young genetics researcher at the University of Michigan, James Wilson, took aim at one of the most common ones—cystic fibrosis.

The gene defect that causes this disease results in an overproduction of sticky mucus that clogs the lungs, damages other organs and usually kills people in their 30s.

The first challenge in gene therapy is figuring out how to get the desired gene inside the patient's cells and into enough cells to make a difference in the disease. Wilson and his colleagues thought they had a great vehicle to deliver the gene: viruses, which excel at infecting cells and can be modified so they do not cause illness.

A second challenge is having the gene stick around so its benefit is long-lasting. Using a retrovirus seemed ideal. This virus not only gets inside a cell but also penetrates the nucleus and stitches its genetic cargo permanently into chromosomes.

But when doctors tried this to treat cystic fibrosis, a biological problem emerged. Only a small fraction of any cells become infected when a virus is introduced into the body. These few infected cells would have to divide and produce more cells containing the virus (and the desired gene it's carrying) for the gene to make a difference in the course of the disease.

But it turned out that lung cells don't divide much, and there are so many of them lining the lungs that they would cover half a football field if stretched flat, Wilson said. The few cells containing the corrected gene were completely inadequate to do the patient any good.

Researchers next tried using something more adept at infecting lung cells—an adenovirus, cause of the common cold. But the immune system attacked the virus and formed antibodies to it, dooming its capacity to deliver its payload—the desired gene—into cells.

"I'm convinced it's an insurmountable problem," and that gene therapy won't work for cystic fibrosis, Wilson said . . . at a genetics seminar at Whitehead.

Volunteer's Death Chills Field

But researchers were not convinced it would not work for other diseases. By 1999, Wilson had moved to the University of Pennsylvania and then led the gene therapy attempt that resulted in the death of Jesse Gelsinger, who had a rare liver disorder that leaves the body unable to clear ammonia from the bloodstream.

The immune response that had simply made earlier adenovirus gene therapies ineffective or short-lived turned out to be fatal in the Arizona teen, triggering massive inflammation in his liver. Clotting factors also were disrupted, more evidence of an overwhelming immune system attack on the adenovirus.

"We weren't even thinking about that. We all thought it was the genes that would cause toxicity," not the virus, Wilson said.

Gelsinger's death led to more regulation, suspension of the work by Wilson and many others at the University of Pennsylvania, and a chilling effect on the entire field.

At a cancer research convention in New Orleans in March 2001, Philip Noguchi, who oversees gene therapy for the FDA, said that applications to do gene therapy had dropped 50 percent in 2000, and that patients were reluctant to participate in experiments.

"The public has lost confidence in this area, there's no doubt about that. We're trying to win it back," Noguchi said.

Meanwhile, other researchers were still using retroviruses for gene therapy, including French doctors who used them on nine children born with "bubble boy" disease, an immune system deficiency that's usually fatal within the first year of life.

Another Setback

That experiment had been considered the first slam-dunk success for gene therapy until last year [2002], when two of the children developed a leukemia-like condition caused by the corrective gene accidentally activating a cancer gene.

Scientists had long feared such an effect because they cannot control where in a person's chromosomes a retrovirus will insert the good gene it is delivering.

Dozens of gene therapy experiments in the U.S. using retroviruses were put on hold. Those that have been allowed to proceed are now moving with great caution and additional guidelines to try to ensure patient safety.

"The challenges of gene delivery are so much more difficult that many originally imagined," said Daley, of the Whitehead Institute.

Its usefulness as a treatment for some diseases also is being questioned. For instance, many researchers now doubt that it will defeat cancer, a disease involving many genes and many pathways that affect how cells turn malignant, multiply and spread.

"It probably will never work" for cancer, said Tyler Jacks, director of the MIT Center for Cancer Research.

"Trying to block pathways is a lot harder than augmenting one," agreed Doug Losordo, a Tufts University doctor who succeeded Isner as director of the gene therapy experiments at St. Elizabeth's Medical Center in suburban Boston where Bettin, the Beloit woman, was treated.

Isner, the program's pioneer, died suddenly of heart problems at the age of 53 two years ago, just after the National Institutes of Health awarded a $10 million grant to expand his gene therapy experiments because results were so encouraging.

Progress with Heart Patients

Those experiments revolve patients with inoperable heart problems and diabetics with neuropathy, painful and irreversible blockages in the nerves of the leg. They're given a gene that makes vascular endothelial growth factor, or VEGF, a substance that spurs new blood vessel growth.

Two things have helped these experiments succeed where others have failed. First, it's not necessary to get the gene into all or even most cells to help the patient. Just getting enough to form some new blood vessels eases the shortage of blood to the heart or leg.

Researchers also used a different method to deliver the gene—a molecular Baggie called a plasmid—instead of a virus. The only side effects have been some swelling at the site of injections.

Other researchers are trying to use a much smaller virus, adeno-associated virus, which causes no known disease, to do gene therapy.

As for the 4-year-old girl and another child who became the nation's first gene therapy patients in 1990, "both of them are still alive, doing reasonably well," but aren't cured and have needed about 10 more gene therapy treatments to keep their disease in check, said Wivel, the former NIH official.

Wilson, who paid a great personal and professional price for his early work on gene therapy, still believes in its value and says people need to be more patient to allow the science to mature.

"If the way you view the field is clinical applications, you'll probably be pretty disappointed" at where things stand now, he said.

Setbacks such as the Gelsinger death have taught valuable lessons, he added.

"As tragic as this was, I think we've redirected gene therapy and gene research," Wilson said. "We're a lot smarter about how to deploy the technology."

CHAPTER 4

The Ethics of Gene Therapy

Ethical Issues Surrounding Gene Therapy

By Catherine Baker

The advent of gene therapy raises a variety of ethical questions. In the following selection, Catherine Baker explores a number of hypothetical situations, philosophical questions, and actual dilemmas involving gene therapy. Among these is the question of whether gene therapy that tampers with a family's gene line threatens to undermine the uniqueness of the individual. For example, gene therapy might prevent a person from passing on genes that would make his or her child albino. Stopping defective genes being passed on is a process called germ line therapy, which effectively changes people who have not been been born yet. The prospect of altering future generations without their consent has led many people to oppose germ line therapy, Baker says. Even if it is ethical to make genetic interventions to prevent an albino, Baker points out that society must decide if it should invest its resources in doing so. Catherine Baker is a Maryland-based writer and editor who has worked on several books for the American Association for the Advancement of Science.

Martin came home from school the other day with a black eye and broken glasses. Another boy had called him a freak and punched him.

Martin is albino, which means that his skin has no color. He is very pale and his hair is white. His eyes are pink and he doesn't see very well.

Martin's mother loves her son very much just the way he is. But when she sees other children tease him, she wishes he were not so different. If he weren't, then perhaps he wouldn't be picked on so much. It makes her wonder why everyone can't be the same.

Do you ever wonder about this yourself? If it were up to you, would you want everyone to be alike?

The world is filled with nearly 6 billion people, but each and every one of us is different from everybody else. Only you have your combination of looks, personality, and behavior. As the saying goes, they broke the mold when you were made! There is *no one* in the world exactly like you. At the same time, you have traits, or ways of looking, thinking, and being, that you share with some other people on earth. For example, you may look like your father or share your mother's sense of humor.

You also have traits that you share with *every* other person on earth. For example, every person has blood, lungs, and a brain. All things considered, you are more like every other person on earth than you are different from them.

Today, powerful computers and other modern research tools are helping scientists learn a great deal more, at a much faster pace. They are figuring out how genes work to do what they do. And they are uncovering the functions of specific genes.

These discoveries are teaching us a great deal about the genetic instructions that construct and operate the human body. This new information will give us new opportunities to control the destiny of our bodies. But at the same time, it will force us to face new and sometimes difficult choices. Some of these choices will have to be made by individuals or families. Other choices will be made by all of us together, as a society.

Questions Raised by Genetic Treatments

To get an idea of the many choices that come with the new genetic information, consider Martin, the boy who is albino. Martin is albino because his genes do not give the right instructions for his body's production of pigment, the dye that colors the skin, eyes, and hair. The result is that Martin is very pale. He must avoid the sun because he is at high risk of sunburn and skin cancer. Strong light hurts his eyes, and his vision is poor, so he needs glasses.

Suppose researchers discover a way to treat Martin's genes so that they give the proper instructions for producing pigment. This kind of genetic treatment may be possible someday. It would mean that Martin's skin and eyes would regain color. He no longer would have to stay out of the sun all the time. Plus, he wouldn't stand out from other children. These changes could make a big difference in Martin's life.

Do you think Martin should have the genetic treatment? In other words, do you think being albino is a medical problem that needs fixing? Or would you say the treatment is more along the lines of a nose job or face-lift—something nice, but not necessary? Your answers to these questions are important, because genetic treatment could be expensive. Should health insurance pay for it? Maybe you say yes. However, the cost of this treatment for people who are albino may drive up the cost of health insurance for everyone. Would that change your answer?

Many Difficult Choices

Think about the choices Martin's mother would have to make. If she loves Martin the way he is, how does she explain a decision to have him treated? But if *he* is unhappy with the way he is, how does she explain a decision *not* to treat him? Also, many medical treatments have side effects. What level of risk is acceptable? Perhaps when Martin grows up, he will decide that he wants to prevent his children from having the problem he has had. He may decide to have any baby of his tested before it is born, to make sure it is not albino. If it is, he and his wife could choose to have an abortion and try again. What do you think of this choice?

Adoption is another choice Martin and his wife could make, instead of risking bearing children who are albino. With adoption, the children would not be their own, genetically. But Martin and his wife could raise the children as their own, and they would not be albino. What do you think of this choice?

It's possible that when Martin grows up, he will be comfortable with how he looks. He may not care whether his children are born albino. In fact, he may even prefer it because then they would look more like him. What do you think about this? Do you think it is wise to let children into the world with problem skin and poor eyesight if we know how to keep this from happening? Should Martin be prevented from having children who are albino? Who are we to say no to him?

Finally, there is the question of where society should put its time and money. Perhaps along with research into the treatment of genetic conditions, we should put equal effort into teaching children (and adults) to accept those who are different. What do you think? These questions are just the "tip of the iceberg" when it comes to genetic research. There are many more. One way to explore the topic is to look at it in terms of the ethical, legal, and social issues. Ethical issues concern what is moral or right. Legal issues concern the protections that laws or regulations should provide. And social issues concern how society as a whole (and individuals in society) will be affected by events.

Another Troubling Case

Dr. Lu has two patients with the same problem, but she isn't sure if she should treat them both. The patients, Tim and Rico, are seven-year-old boys who are very short for their age.

Tim will never grow much taller than 5 feet because his body does not produce enough of a hormone needed to grow. When he is an adult, Tim will be much shorter than his mother and father, who are both closer to 6 feet.

Rico will never grow much taller than 5 feet either. Rico will be short because he has inherited his body build from his parents, who are both about five feet tall.

Researchers have used genetic engineering to produce a growth hormone. Both sets of parents want this growth hormone to be prescribed for their sons to help them grow taller. They want this because they feel that there are many advantages to being tall.

Dr. Lu realizes that genes play a role in the height each child will reach. Tim will be short because of a single mutation in one gene that instructs for the production of a growth hormone. Rico will be short due to the many genes he inherited from two short parents. Despite this difference, the end result for both boys will be the same.

Dr. Lu is thinking about prescribing the hormone for Tim, but not for Rico. However, she wonders if she is being fair. If you were Dr. Lu, what would you do?

Limitations of Gene Therapy

Treating disorders by altering genes is called gene therapy. It will work something like this. When you have an illness, your doctor will determine whether the problem is caused by a mutated gene that is giving out faulty instructions for the production of a needed protein. If so, new DNA will be inserted into some of your cells. This new DNA will correct the gene's instruction for making the protein. If the treatment is successful, the repaired gene in these cells will go to work, giving out the proper instructions so that the protein is produced.

It is too early to tell whether these treatments will work. Hundreds of research trials are under way using gene therapy. None has yet been able to claim complete success, although a lot of valuable things are being learned. Even so, gene therapy is still so experimental that it is being tried only on patients who have diseases for which there are no other cures.

It's also important to realize that gene therapy may never work for a wide range of health problems. It may be too difficult to use genetic therapy for disorders that involve the actions of many genes. Also, for many health problems in which genes are involved, the genes are only partly responsible for what's wrong. In such cases, gene therapy may be only part of the solution. Gene therapy also may be of little use in treating medical problems that have no genetic cause, such as broken bones or wounds caused by an accident.

Germ-Line Therapy

The kind of gene therapy we have talked about so far will be for people who are already born. That is, it will fix some of the genes at work in a part of a person's body. It will not affect the genes that a person passes on to the next generation. However, even that may be possible some day. The kind of treatment that could change the genes you pass on to your children is called germ-line therapy.

Researchers are figuring out how to alter the DNA in your germ cells. If they succeed, this means that they would be able to alter the DNA that is copied and passed on through your eggs (if you are female) or your sperm (if you are male). With germ-line therapy, genes could be "corrected" in the egg or sperm you are using to conceive. The child that results would be spared certain genetic problems that might otherwise have occurred. It may even be possible someday to use germ-line therapy to remove a disorder from your family tree forever. Your children would not inherit the problem gene. Neither would your grandchildren or your great-grandchildren. Germ-line therapy is a long way off. However, it already is very controversial. In fact, it is so controversial, that the

U.S. government currently does not allow federal funds to be used for germ-line experiments on human patients.

Most people who have thought about germ-line therapy do not oppose the idea of using it to help families rid themselves of the genes for terrible diseases. However, they are concerned because making changes to the germ line of one person can affect many people who are that person's descendants. They say that perhaps it is not right to make changes to a germ line, because some of the people who will be affected are not even born yet and therefore cannot give their consent. An even bigger concern is that making changes to germ cells could disrupt the development of the embryo or fetus in unexpected ways. For these reasons, most people feel that germ-line therapy should not be used until we fully understand its long-term effects and have addressed the ethical questions it raised.

Ethical Questions Go Beyond Gene Therapy

Although gene therapy is still experimental, in other ways genetic research already has changed how medicine is practiced. This is because of the genetically engineered drugs that are now available through biotechnology.

Human growth hormone is one of the medical products that can now be manufactured through genetic engineering. In the past, its only source was recently dead human donors. Getting human growth hormone in this way was difficult and controversial. It also did not recover very much of the hormone. Furthermore, there was a risk that hormones from dead bodies might be contaminated and pass on diseases. With genetic engineering, human growth hormone can now be produced in pure form in large quantities. This has made the hormone more widely available. That's why Dr. Lu faces her decision on treating Tim and Rico, the boys who are both very short. Without treatment, neither boy will end up much over five feet tall. There is nothing unhealthy about being only five feet tall, of course. However, Dr. Lu may feel that Tim should have treatment because his one gene is not working normally. She may even feel that Rico should have treatment because his normal genes will cause him to be abnormally short.

Suppose, however, that Dr. Lu's next patients are children who will grow to be only 5 foot 4 inches or 5 foot 6 inches. If their families want them to be taller, what should she do? Where does she draw the line? It's even possible that as people hear about this growth hormone, they will demand it for their tall children to make them even taller. What will Dr. Lu do for families that want their boys to be seven-foot-tall basketball stars?

No Quick Fix

One thing that Dr. Lu has to consider is that the treatment is not quick and easy. For it to work, the boys will have to receive a great many shots over several years. The treatment appears to have side effects. For example, it may cause bad cases of acne that leave scars. Also, the treatment doesn't guarantee how much the boys will grow. Studies suggest that the treatment works better for children like Tim, who has a single mutated gene responsible for his stunted growth, compared to children like Rico, who has many genes contributing to his short build. Even so, all those years of shots may give Tim a few extra few inches and Rico even less.

Dr. Lu also must consider the fact that the treatment would be performed on children. Genetically engineered drugs are still new. It's possible that there are long-term side effects that no one knows about yet. Since Tim and Rico are children, they can't make the decision themselves. On the other hand, Dr. Lu can't wait until they are adults for them to decide, because the treatment needs to start while they are still growing. So perhaps the decision rests with the parents. Yet before she turns the decision over to them, Dr. Lu must consider one more thing: whether the problem of being short is really a medical problem that deserves treatment. The parents may feel that if their children are taller, they will have more success. The question remains, however: What needs changing, the boys or the idea that short is bad and tall is good?

The Ugly History of Eugenics

Genetic research is uncovering new ways to treat, cure, and even prevent many kinds of diseases and disorders. However, it is quite likely that the new techniques will be used in ways that don't always have to do with health. In Dr. Lu's story, two families wanted a genetically engineered drug for their children not because the children were sick, but because they wanted them to be taller. Genetically engineered drugs, gene therapy, and germ-line therapy could open the door for lots of people to change how they or their children look. People may seek genetic treatments that will make them look younger, have more hair, or lose weight. If researchers ever figure out how genes control for behavior and ability, people may try to use that knowledge, too, for example, to improve their I.Q. or their athletic ability. There is nothing new about people wanting to improve themselves. What will be new is the opportunity to use genetic techniques to make those improvements.

There is a word that describes the use of genetic knowledge to improve the human race. The word is eugenics. "Eugenics" comes from a Greek word meaning "wellborn." For many people, the word has a bad ring to it. This is because eugenic ideas often have been used by people to claim that they are better than others.

That is what happened in Nazi Germany. Hundreds of thousands of people were sterilized, and millions more were killed, in concentration camps because the Nazis wanted to "purify" the German race. They targeted Jews and also Gypsies, homosexuals, and many others. Many of these people were victims of cruel and inhumane experiments designed to prove Nazi eugenic theories.

Even before the Nazis came to power, however, eugenic ideas were very popular in the United States and Europe. Many people in the first half of the 1900s believed that crime, poverty, and other social problems were the fault of people with "bad blood." They also believed that people of "poor stock" were reproducing more quickly than people of "good stock," leading to the decline of the human race.

The people who held these ideas considered themselves to have "good blood." They were for the most part well to do, educated, white, Protestant, and descended from northern Europeans. People with "bad blood" were people who were different from them— poor, uneducated, of color, Catholic or Jewish, and descended from southern Europeans.

Scientists' Role in Eugenics

Some people who held eugenic ideas also were scientists. These scientists conducted research to support their theories. For the most part, their research was badly done and affected by their beliefs about the kinds of people who were good or bad. Even so, many states in the U.S. adopted laws to control "overbreeding" by people of poor stock. For example, thousands of prostitutes and black women were sterilized on the grounds that they were "feebleminded."

Eugenic ideas are popular even today. China has a law that forbids mentally retarded people from marrying if they have not been sterilized. Singapore offers cash rewards to well-educated women who have babies.

In the U.S., the eugenics laws from the first half of the century are no longer on the books. However, the beliefs still persist. One new way these beliefs are expressed is in the idea that poor people are poor because they have poor genes. This idea is not based on good science, but that does not prevent the idea from catching on.

Could Eugenics Return?

Some people fear that once we have the tools to tinker with our genes, we may be tempted to use them to design a "super" race of human beings. As a practical matter, this will probably never be possible. It's one thing to use gene therapy to get rid of an unwanted gene or two. It's a whole lot more to pick and choose the whole range of genes that make an ideal person.

First of all, you would have to decide what is the ideal. Then you would have to figure out which different genes come into play to make that ideal. And then you would have to figure out how to raise all the children so that they grow up to be ideal. Even if you could solve all those issues, you would still need the political power to make it happen. A grand plan to "improve" the human race would involve the government in personal childbearing and child-rearing choices. This would certainly be opposed by many and difficult to enforce.

So we may never make a "super" race. But in more limited ways, we may be able to shape our future. We may be able to spare ourselves and our descendants from terrible diseases and disorders. We also may be able to select some of the traits of our children. But do we want to? We also need to think about whether these choices will be available to everyone. It probably won't matter too much if some people don't get to select the eye color of their children. However, it will matter a great deal if some day only poor people suffer from terrible genetic disorders because they are the only ones who cannot afford genetic medicines and gene therapy.

We also need to worry about whether genetic technology will make us less accepting of people who are different. For example, if it is possible to predict and prevent the birth of a child with a gene-related disorder, how will we react to children we meet who have that disorder? Will we think, Why is this child alive? Will we think, Why didn't the parents "do something" to prevent the child's condition? Will we resent the medical and special education costs spent on the child? Will we put pressure on parents not to have "defective" children?

One of the important beliefs upon which this country was built is the idea that we are all "created equal." We know from the study of our genes that we are indeed very much alike. But we are not genetically equal. And no matter how much we tinker with our genes, we never will be. However, that doesn't mean that we don't all have equal rights. It's important to remember that what we believe in is as important as what science allows us to do.

Your Genes, Your Choices

We have talked about the many ways that genetic research is changing the world we live in. It's truly exciting. It's also overwhelming. You may feel that you have little control over the way that genetic research will be used, for good or for bad. But you do have power. The way that society uses its knowledge of genetics will be shaped by the everyday choices its citizens make.

You help shape what happens through the way you express your beliefs and opinions and by the actions you take. You also affect what happens through your community efforts, working for the passage of laws or electing leaders who believe as you do. . . . Now you have the choice to remain informed. You have the choice to use your knowledge when making personal decisions that involve the use of genetic research. And you have the choice to participate when issues involving genetics are raised in your community.

A Legal Perspective on Genetic Ethics

By Maxwell J. Mehlman

Gene therapy raises a wide variety of thorny issues that courts will be called on to decide, says Maxwell J. Mehlman in the selection that follows. One question that might go to the courts to decide is whether or not private health insurers or government programs such as Medicare should be required to pay for gene therapy when indicated. Mehlman says that past court decisions do not point to a clear outcome on such questions. Some of the most difficult issues in both legal and ethical terms will be posed by enhancement therapies that parents may want to provide to their children. Finding the balance between parental freedom and the best interests of children will become increasingly complex as the variety of options grows. Assuring that both the poor and the affluent have access to gene therapy will likely be difficult as well, Mehlman explains. Mehlman is director of the Law-Medicine Center at the Case Western Reserve University School of Law and a professor of bioethics at the university's medical school. A former Rhodes scholar, he earned a juris doctor degree at Yale University. Mehlman is coeditor of the *Encyclopedia of Ethical, Legal and Policy Issues in Biotechnology.*

Gene therapy already is a reality. Hundreds of clinical trials are underway to test the safety and efficacy of gene therapy to treat disorders such as cystic fibrosis and Parkinson's disease.

So far, these new technologies are limited to producing so-called "somatic" effects in patients—that is, effects that do not al-

Maxwell J. Mehlman, "The Human Genome Project and the Courts: Gene Therapy and Beyond," *Judicature*, vol. 83, November/December 1999. Copyright © 1999 by American Judicature Society. Reproduced by permission.

ter reproductive cells and therefore that would not be passed on to the patient's offspring. But studies have been proposed in which genetic manipulations would change the DNA inside eggs or sperm. These so-called "germ line gene therapies" introduce the possibility of eliminating genetically-related diseases in succeeding generations.

The future holds the prospect of even more daring genetic manipulations. The Human Genome Project will provide scientists with the data and tools to identify and understand the basis of genetic diseases and disorders, as well as other genetically-related traits. This creates the possibility of genetic interventions to enhance nondisease traits, for example, to increase strength, stamina, and perhaps even intelligence. Nor are these enhancement technologies just in the realm of science fiction. Scientists have begun to use gene transfer technologies to enhance the immune systems of advanced cancer- and HIV-infected patients, and they are experimentally transferring "foreign" genes (i.e., not one's own) into healthy subjects in search of new mechanisms to deliver gene therapies to patients.

These new technologies will create a host of difficult, often unprecedented, ethical and legal controversies, many of which will find their way to the courts for resolution.

Access Issues

New gene therapies will prevent, cure, or more effectively treat many diseases that previously were unavoidable, incurable, or untreatable, or that responded to treatment only incompletely or was accompanied by numerous side effects. Gene therapy therefore will be in great demand. If it provides a cheaper alternative to existing medical interventions, it will be embraced by patients and readily offered by managed care plans and other third-party payers, such as Medicare and Medicaid. But in many cases, a gene therapy will increase rather than decrease health care costs. For example, it might be a more effective but also more expensive treatment than before. Or, it might target a disease for which there were no previous medical options, and thus no treatment cost. In these cases, third-party payers will resist paying for these new technologies, and this will lead to disputes that come before the courts.

In the case of private health insurance plans, the conflict will be over the scope of coverage. This is an issue with which courts are familiar, although not one that they necessarily have resolved consistently or with ease. It requires judges and juries to examine the language of the policy to see if the treatment in question—in this case, gene therapy—is explicitly excluded from coverage. Most likely, the treatment is not mentioned specifically in the policy (because of plan administrators' worries over the application of the expressio unius est exclusio alterius doctrine, which holds that when a list includes specific items, items not included are presumed to be excluded), and the insurer contends that the therapy is excluded under general policy language because it is not "medically necessary" or because it is "experimental."

The courts have wrestled with the meaning of these terms in cases involving other new medical interventions, such as bone marrow transplants for breast cancer. The outcomes in these cases are mixed, in part because they depend on the language of specific health insurance policies in question, but also because some judges and juries are more sympathetic to patients and their families, while others are more concerned with the insurers' need to control their costs. Nor can the courts simply rely on whether or not the gene therapy has been approved by the Food and Drug Administration; although most gene therapies will require FDA approval before they may be marketed in interstate commerce, physicians lawfully may recommend to patients an approved therapy for a purpose for which it has not been approved.

The Role of Managed Care

Increasingly aggressive efforts by managed care organizations to lower costs have given rise to one particular type of coverage decision that adversely affects an enrollee's chances of obtaining access to gene therapies: *prospective utilization review.* Under prospective utilization review, a health care provider must obtain the plan's agreement to cover a service before it is given to the patient; otherwise, the plan will not pay for the service even if in fact it would be covered under the plan. The process of challenging a plan's refusal to cover a service can be time-consuming, and all the while the patient is being denied access to the treatment. (In contrast, under the older, less aggressive form of management known as *retrospective utilization review*, the provider furnishes the service first and then submits a claim for reimbursement. If the plan determines that the service is not covered, the patient may be forced to pay the provider, but at least the patient has received the benefit of the treatment.)

Coverage disputes also arise under government entitlement programs such as Medicare and Medicaid. Medicare law, for example, excludes coverage of services that are "not medically necessary or appropriate." New gene therapies would not be considered medically necessary if they were still being investigated for safety and efficacy.

Both private health insurance plans and public programs are establishing administrative grievance procedures for resolving coverage controversies. An increasing number of private plans are requiring enrollees to arbitrate these disputes, a practice that has provoked varying judicial responses. As state legislatures move to regulate managed care plans, they are enacting laws that mandate the adoption of grievance procedures for coverage disputes, often requiring that the disputes be resolved by external bodies. The federal government has established administrative procedures for grievances involving Medicare and Medicaid HMO's [health maintenance organizations]. The Patients Bill of Rights, although currently stalled in Congress, would create an elaborate administrative appeals procedure. Often, these administrative measures by their terms preclude judicial review. Over time, courts therefore may find themselves less involved in disputes over coverage.

Human Experimentation Disputes

The adoption of a new medical technique typically is preceded by extensive scientific studies to establish its safety and efficacy. In the case of new gene therapies, these studies would be required by the FDA under its authority to regulate drugs and biologic products. Disputes may arise over the ethics of conducting these investigations, particularly on the appropriateness of experimenting on children and fetuses, and in the case of germ-line therapies, on human embryos (germ-line therapy involves altering DNA of early-stage embryos so that the alteration occurs in its reproductive cells). Courts may be called on to resolve conflicts between the wishes of researchers, parents, and the subjects. For example, to what extent does a parent have the authority to enroll a child in a gene therapy experiment when there is no direct benefit to the child?

Courts also will be called upon to settle disputes over proprietary interests in new therapies. Disputes between inventors and research sponsors may involve the application of traditional intellectual property doctrines to novel genetic technologies. More unusual controversies, involving both novel legal doctrines and novel technologies, are likely to arise between experimenters and their subjects, such as is illustrated by the approach taken by the California Supreme Court on the commercialization of cell lines in *Moore v. Regents of the University of California* (1991). In that case, the court held that researchers must inform patients of the commercial motivation behind their research, presumably to give patients a chance to negotiate an economic benefit for themselves.

Standard of Care

New gene therapy technologies raise complex questions concerning the appropriate standard of care for health care professionals. Physicians who fail to recommend a new technology to their patients may run the risk of malpractice liability, even though the technology has not yet become incorporated into standard practice. The question remains open when awareness of a new technique has sufficiently diffused throughout the community of health professionals that the technique must be offered to patients as an alternative to more traditional therapies. On the other hand, physicians who recommend a new technique before it becomes standard practice must be careful to disclose to patients that the technique is still experimental, and to obtain the patients' informed consent to employ an experimental approach.

These liability risks accompany all medical innovations. What may set gene therapy apart is the unprecedented potential that it may offer, for example, the ability to successfully combat genetic illnesses that were hitherto unresponsive to treatment. As a consequence, patients may demand access to gene therapy when they first hear about it, even though it is still in the early stages of testing, and they may seek to hold health professionals legally responsible for failing to provide them with the nascent treatment. This may embroil the courts in disputes similar to the celebrated but singular case of *Helling v. Carey* (1974), in which the court disregarded expert testimony that providing patients with a new test for detecting glaucoma was not yet required by the ophthalmologist's standard of care.

The rapid pace of gene therapy development will impose liability risks particularly on two groups of health professionals: primary care physicians and genetic counselors. Primary care physicians are vulnerable because, compared with physicians who specialize in genetic medicine, they may not be as familiar with new gene therapies. Yet they will serve as the gateway to these therapies, particularly if managed care continues to require patients to obtain referrals to specialists from their primary care physicians before the plan will pay for specialty care. Patients who are harmed when inadequately informed primary care physicians fail to refer them to genetic counselors or gene therapy specialists may bring malpractice actions. If the patients suspect that the primary care physicians' failure to refer them is motivated in part by the financial pressures exerted on the physicians by the patient's managed care plan, the patient may attempt to sue the physician for breach of fiduciary duty as well as for malpractice. Alternatively, the patient may sue the managed care plan, either under a theory of vicarious liability (if the physician appears to be employed by the plan) or corporate negligence. . . .

Malpractice actions against genetic counselors may find their way to the courts as these health care professionals become more integrated into primary patient care in response to the development of new genetic tests and therapies. Genetic counselors, who typically are not physicians, often will serve as a layer of expertise between primary care physicians and physician geneticists. In this role, they will be responsible for educating patients at risk for genetic ailments about the benefits and risks of new genetic technologies. Not only will they have to inform and advise patients about the complex matrix of individual genetic risk factors revealed by an expanding array of genetic tests, and to help patients compare the medical benefits and risks of various gene therapies and alternative treatments; they also will be the primary source of patient information about the nonmedical costs of accessing genetic technologies, including the risks of insurance and employment discrimination.

Enhancement Therapies

As mentioned at the outset of this article, the revolution in human genetics will extend beyond identifying and preventing or treating genetic ailments. The same techniques that respond to genetic disorders also will be applicable to nondisease traits. Currently much work is underway to identify the proteins that genes "code for" in order to correct protein imbalances that produce illness. The same process can be used to produce drugs that affect any other protein-dependent characteristic, not just those that are regarded as illnesses. Similarly, gene transfer technology that will be used to remove errant DNA or to install healthy DNA also will be able to manipulate DNA for other purposes.

At this point it is not known how many nondisease human characteristics are, at least in part, inherited. But research already has confirmed that certain traits that many would consider fundamental to personal well-being and social success—traits such as beauty, strength, and intelligence—are substantially influenced by a person's genetic endowment. Many of these traits probably are "multifactorial"—that is, the result of the interaction of numerous individual genes and with environmental factors. Altering the function of one of these genes may have undesired effects on other physical or mental characteristics. Eventually, however, research is likely to reveal techniques for successfully "improving" or "enhancing" a person's nondisease genetic traits. This raises a host of problems that will begin to confront the judicial system in the next century. I want to discuss a few of the most challenging issues here.

Parental Authority

It is a truism that parents typically want to give their children the best chance in life that they can. Indeed, some parents seem to know no bounds, such as the mother who was sentenced to 10 years in jail for plotting to murder a popular junior high school cheerleader so that her daughter could fill the vacancy on the cheerleading squad.

Parents not only put their children in private schools and pay for piano lessons; increasingly they turn to medical interventions to give their kids a perceived advantage over others. An endocrinologist reports being asked by parents to prescribe human growth hormone to their child so that she could gain the two inches in height needed to make her an irresistible candidate for college volleyball scholarships. A recent report in the press says that a growing number of parents in California and other Sunbelt states are giving their daughters breast implants as high school graduation presents.

The question that the courts will be forced to struggle with is whether there is a legal limit to the authority of parents to manipulate the genetic characteristics of their children. One way this issue will arise is when parents give their children drugs to improve performance in sports competitions or mental achievement tests. Even if these practices are not expressly forbidden by law or by the private legal rules governing the activity, the possible health risks may subject parents to charges of child endangerment. Similar doubts about parental fitness would arise if parents agreed to let their children participate in experiments to determine the safety and efficacy of enhancement products. In none of these cases, moreover, would the parents be able to hide behind the shield of religious freedom, as they often can now in making questionable treatment decisions for their children.

Yet parents are not likely to wait until a child is born in order to attempt to influence its genetic inheritance, including its inheritance of nondisease characteristics. The availability of genetic tests will open the door to several types of genetic enhancements that will take place much earlier. The first of these is *pre-conception enhancement*, in which decisions about whether or not and with whom to conceive a child would be made on the basis of pre-conception genetic testing. Just as some people now test themselves to avoid conceiving a child with another person who is a "carrier" for a recessive genetic disorder, prospective mates in the future could test themselves to ascertain if they were likely to produce offspring who were "superior" in terms of nondisease characteristics. Unsatisfactory results would lead to decisions not to marry or not to conceive, at least not without employing genetic manipulations to improve the genetic profile of the offspring.

Another form of genetic enhancement stemming from genetic testing would be *enhancement via selective abortion*. Fetuses would be tested in utero and those that did not match up to parents' expectations would be aborted, just as fetuses currently might be aborted if they tested positive for abnormalities or incurable diseases. An alternative to selective abortion would be embryo selection for enhancement, which combines genetic testing with in vitro fertilization so that embryos were tested before they were implanted in the womb, and only embryos with advantageous characteristics were implanted.

Finally, and most dramatically, an early-stage embryo might be genetically altered prior to implantation, with DNA inserted or deleted to produce desired traits in the resulting child. If performed at an early-enough stage of embryonic development, the alteration would affect all subsequent fetal cells, including germ cells—that is, those that became eggs or sperm. This would result in *germ-cell enhancement*, in which genetic changes would be passed on when the enhanced individual reproduced.

Some of these actions undoubtedly lie within the realm of constitutionally protected personal autonomy and reproductive freedom, for example, the decision about whom to marry based on genetic testing. Other activities may not be so clearly protected. Some scholars argue, for example, that the state has a legitimate interest in regulating selective abortion and embryo selection when performed for enhancement purposes, even though parents have a constitutional right to abort and perhaps even to select embryos for implantation when they do so for medical reasons, such as to avoid the birth of a child with a genetic illness.

State Versus Parents

An interesting question is what the state's interest would be in regulating parental access to genetic enhancement for their children. The interest might be the need to prevent harm to the future child, similar to the justification offered for government actions to prohibit illegal drug use by pregnant women that threatens the health of the fetus. Yet assuming that genetic enhancement techniques are developed that do not physically harm the child, the state would have to rely on less tangible forms of harm. Some commentators have suggested that genetic enhancement interferes with the child's right to genetic autonomy—that children deserve a genetic endowment free from parental manipulation. Yet parents invariably manipulate their children's futures once they are born. What is so different about doing so before the child is born, assuming that the manipulation is beneficial to the child?

A stronger basis for upholding governmental restrictions on parents' ability genetically to enhance their children might be the negative impact of genetic enhancement on our democratic political system. Genetic enhancement is likely to be accessible only to wealthier families, since it is not likely to be covered by public or private health insurance plans.

Wealth Rules

Assuming that genetic enhancement is effective at improving personal traits that correlate with social success, those who can afford to purchase genetic enhancements will gain significant social advantages, and the ability to genetically enhance their children, particularly the use of germ-line enhancements that are passed on to succeeding generations, could create a "genobility" with an unassailable lock on power and privilege. The threat that this poses is more than just a philosophical objection to social inequality; it is a threat to the fundamental belief in equality of opportunity that sustains our political system in the face of frank disparities of wealth, privilege, and power. If, as the result of wealth-based access to genetic enhancement, society becomes divided into genetic haves (the enhanced) and have nots (the unenhanced), the possibility of upward social mobility will be seen as illusory. In the face of such a hardened class structure, the underclass is likely to rebel, in turn provoking anti-democratic repression by the genetic upper class. Even if a stable political system eventually emerged, it would not resemble Western liberal democracy.

Avoiding such a fate is a sufficiently compelling state interest to justify a wide range of restrictions on parental enhancement of offspring, as well as substantial limitations on the freedom of adults to purchase enhancements for themselves. For example, the law might legitimately ban the use of germ-line genetic enhancements, and it might allow persons to purchase somatic enhancements for themselves only on condition that they make an enforceable commitment to employ their advantages for social and not just personal benefit, in much the same way that we license professionals such as doctors and lawyers.

No matter what approach society takes to genetic enhancements, some individuals undoubtedly will obtain them—whether by becoming licensed or by purchasing them in an unregulated free market or through black or gray markets in a highly restricted system of access. These individuals will gain significant advantages over unenhanced persons with whom they interact or compete. How should the law respond to the potential unfairness of these interactions?

The law is no stranger to imbalances between interacting parties. In certain situations, courts are called upon to enforce bans on such interactions, such as the private rules that prohibit the use of performance-enhancing drugs in the Olympics or other sports competitions, or the securities laws that ban trading on inside information. In other situations, the law requires the advantaged party to disgorge the advantage to the benefit of the other party, such as by requiring disclosure of information to correct a material mistake by the other party to a contract negotiation. The doctrine of unconscionability allows courts to void a contract if the outcome, resulting from an imbalance of market power or information between the parties, seems too unfair. In still other contexts, the law eliminates the arm's length nature of the transaction, making the advantaged party a fiduciary who must act in the other party's best interests. Yet in some instances, the rules seem blind to the potential unfairness. SAT scores for college applicants are not weighted in terms of IQ, despite the obvious unfairness. Shorter basketball players are not allowed to shoot from stepladders.

These varying responses of the law make it difficult to predict how courts will respond to the unfairness created by genetic enhancements. Yet it seems certain that, at least in some cases, courts will feel compelled to level the playing field.

Differing Standards?

A final illustration of the potential impact of genetic enhancement on the courts is its effect on the standard of care to which people are expected to adhere when they create risks of injury to one another. Should an enhanced person be held to the standard of care of an ordinary reasonable person, or to the standard of an enhanced person? An obvious answer might be that, if enhanced persons ought to be better at avoiding accidents than unenhanced persons, then the enhanced persons should be held to an enhanced person's standard of care. In other words, they should not escape liability by showing that they met a reasonable person's standard of care when, by virtue of their enhancements, they ought to have done better.

Automobile drivers with enhanced vision who run over children, for example, should not be heard to argue that, although they could have seen the child in enough time to stop, they were not negligent since an ordinary person would not have been able to stop in time. This seems to be the answer that the Restatement of Torts would give, since section 289 states that, at least in regard to appreciating the risk created by one's behavior, an actor must use "such superior attention, perception, memory, knowledge, intelligence, and judgment as the actor himself has."

A good argument can be made, however, that when it comes to reducing the costs of accidents, we indeed ought to hold an enhanced person to the lower standard of an ordinary "reasonable" person. The reason is that by not penalizing them with an enhanced person's standard, we will encourage more people to enhance themselves, thereby reducing accidents simply because, as a result of their better vision or reflexes or intelligence, enhanced people are better at avoiding them.

The broad scope of the issues mentioned in this article—from automobile accidents to altering the genes of future generations—demonstrates the breadth of the impact that gene therapy and related technologies will have on our society. They will challenge conventional notions of illness, insurance, personal worth, and desert, and the limits of governmental control over individual freedom and parental discretion. Ultimately the courts will decide how far the law can go in response to these challenges. One thing is certain: the society that emerges will look very different from our own.

Playing God:
Genes and
Theology

By Audrey R. Chapman

The responses of faith communities to gene therapies could have a profound effect on future regulation of such technologies. In the excerpts that follow, theological ethicist Audrey R. Chapman says that the overall reaction of religious communities to gene therapy has been positive, but she notes that few offer blanket acceptance. For example, most religious analysis rejects the idea of using gene therapy to improve healthy children by enhancing mental or physical abilities, according to Chapman. The challenge that lies ahead, she indicates, is for theologians to sort out how genetic technologies will change conceptions about the human spirit or soul. Additionally, she says, religions need to develop more specific ethical guidelines to help people decide what types of gene therapy are morally acceptable in their communities. Chapman was director of the American Association for the Advancement of Science's Program of Dialogue on Science, Ethics and Religion until October 2002. She holds a doctorate in government from Columbia University and graduate degrees in theology and ethics from New York Theological Seminary and Union Theological Seminary, and continues to direct the Association's Science and Human Rights Program.

T he religious community has generally had a positive attitude toward genetic science. "Playing God" has come to be used as a shorthand for concerns that it is inappropriate for humans to change the way other living organisms or human beings are constituted. The term conveys the view that engaging in ge-

Audrey R. Chapman, "Genetic Engineering and Theology: Exploring the Interconnections," *Theology Today*, vol. 59, April 1, 2002, p. 71. Copyright © 2002 by *Theology Today*. Reproduced by permission of the publisher and the author.

netic engineering amounts to usurping the creative prerogative of God. Ironically, this claim originates from and is generally used by secular critics rather than members of the religious community. Christian and Jewish thinkers writing on genetics generally affirm that genetic engineering, at least in principle, does not go beyond the limits of a reasonable dominion over nature. Openness to genetic engineering, particularly among the moral theologians well versed in science, often derives from the realization that nature itself is constantly engaging in a process akin to human genetic engineering, albeit with significant differences. Others believe that our growing genetic knowledge and capabilities reflect God's activity and purposes. According to one theologian, "the purpose of genetic engineering is to expand our ability to participate in God's work of redemption and creation and thereby to glorify God." Another theologian, who proposes that . . . the image of God embedded in the human race be conceptualized in terms of creativity, argues that technological intervention into the cell line of a life form, when oriented toward a beneficent end, can be understood as a legitimate exercise of this God-given human creativity. Others claim that the biblical mandate to humanity to understand and to make something of the creation justifies the technological manipulation of life to serve human welfare.

While generally favorable to genetic science, faith-based sources typically reject a position of unconditional acceptance of scientific achievement that is not tempered by humane and ethical considerations. Religious thinkers and communities have often assumed an important role in attempting to hold genetic research and applications to an ethical standard of evaluation. A 1996 policy statement on genetics of the National Council of Churches of Christ in the U.S.A., for example, states, "We cannot agree with those who assert that scientific inquiry and research should acknowledge no limits. All that can be known need not be known if in advance it clearly appears that the process for gaining such knowledge violates the sanctity of human life."

Testing in the Light of Faith

Many religious thinkers place greater priority on anticipating and preventing potential problems than on favoring technologies and applications because they may bring future benefits. One author aptly characterizes this presumption of caution as "critical engagement." He explains that Christians generally support genetic science but are required to evaluate any particular genetic discovery or application according to criteria informed by faith and Christian sources. I think this characterization also fits many religious thinkers in other traditions as well.

Human applications of genetic science raise complicated sets of issues. Given a presumption of caution, it is essential to ascertain whether a specific intervention (or omission, exception, policy, or law) is likely to promote or undermine human welfare. Recognizing that many of the issues at hand are complex and that human motives may be ambiguous, how should determinations about appropriate genetic research and applications be made? To do so requires at least the development of a methodology or set of criteria for evaluating whether genetic science is truly in the service of beneficence, the risks involved, and the faith implications of going forward. Unfortunately, few religious sources engage in such a comprehensive evaluation. Nor have religiously oriented ethicists put forward principles to apply in making such determinations. Some of them offer values to take into account, such as the relational nature of human beings and the importance of justice and compassion, but they do not translate these values into middle axioms that can be applied to specific issues. Alternatively, they present a series of relevant questions but little guidance on how to employ them.

Most of the faith-based literature is more intent on interpreting the meaning of genetic discoveries than on offering guidance in this critical issue. To put it another way, these resources sensitize readers to the issues that genetic research and applications raise, but often fail to offer guidelines on how to resolve these dilemmas. The value of these works is usually more in the questions they raise than in the answers they provide. The work on cloning and stem-cell research constitutes something of an exception, but even here religious thinkers, including those from the same communion, sometimes disagree or fail to articulate a well developed theological rationale. . . .

Facing the Tough Issues

Given the value placed on healing and compassion, virtually no ethicist or religious community contests the principle that new genetic knowledge should be used to improve human health and relieve suffering. This is the position in the Jewish and Islamic sources that address the topic, as well as the greater number of Christian religious thinkers and bodies considering genetic therapies. Generally, religious thinkers do not consider somatic or non-inheritable genetic therapies as being different in principle from other forms of medical treatment. Like other experimental medical therapies, the moral calculus often depends on such factors as the potential benefits to the patient, the risks entailed, and the costs and burdens of the treatment.

If anything, the positive inclination of the religious community may be criticized for giving far too little attention to what might be termed the hard issues related to genetic medicine. Although human gene therapy offers potentially effective new treatments, it is and will continue to be quite expensive. Thus, societal investments in genetic research and therapy will come at the cost of foregoing other types of medical research and care. This trade-off is not a trivial issue in a society in which more than forty-one million persons lack even basic medical insurance and the medical services it provides. Moreover, access to gene therapy will likely depend on the ability to pay or to have medical insurance willing to reimburse the costs. As one secular ethicist points out, genetic medicine, "perhaps more than any other biomedical undertaking, raises profound issues of whether all new information is good, whether some medical information is not empowering but disempowering, whether society has the inclination or ability to afford equal access to a powerful new technology, and whether the legal system can deal effectively with the potential for discrimination, limits on autonomy, and political divisiveness of genetic information." The religious community has yet to address many of these issues in a meaningful way.

To date, most of the research and clinical resources have been invested in developing techniques for somatic-cell gene therapies designed to treat or eliminate genetic disease in a specific patient receiving treatment. Recent advances and research in animals, however, are also raising the possibility that scientists may have the technical capacity at some point in the future to modify genes that are transmitted to future generations. Germ or reproductive cells are the body cells that develop into the egg or sperm of a developing organism and convey its inheritable characteristics. In theory, modifying the genes that are transmitted to future generations provides the possibility of economically eliminating the inheritance of some genetically based diseases, rather than re-peating somatic therapy generation after generation. Because germline intervention would be performed at the earliest stage of human development, it offers the potential for preventing irre-versible damage attributable to defective genes before it occurs. Some scientists and ethicists also claim that germline interven-tion is medically necessary to prevent some genetic disorders that cannot be identified through screening and embryo selection pro-cedures. Others anticipate that the ability to correct genetic dis-orders will eliminate the need for therapeutic abortions. Over a long period of time, germline gene transfers could decrease the incidence of certain inherited diseases that currently cause great suffering.

While members of the religious community frequently wel-come therapeutic developments that may conquer or ameliorate serious diseases, they tend, understandably, to have more reser-vations toward proposals to modify the genes that are transmitted to future generations. Writings by religious thinkers frequently raise questions about whether we have the wisdom and ethical commitments that should accompany any efforts to reengineer hu-man nature to assure that it is done in a manner that is equitable, just, and respectful of human dignity. Most religious bodies that have adopted positions on the topic, nevertheless, express caution rather than categorical rejection, often on the grounds of the need for safety and efficacy before proceeding. Some religious thinkers are even more open to contemplating the use of such technologies, provided they are safe and used solely for therapeutic purposes.

A Stand Against Enhancements

Religious thinkers and communities generally oppose efforts to go beyond therapeutic applications of genetic technologies, at-tempts to "enhance" or improve normal human characteristics, such as height or intelligence. A literature is developing, for ex-ample, that warns against efforts to engineer "designer children." Like some secular ethicists, religious thinkers have worried that too great a readiness to attempt to control the genetic inheritance of our offspring will undermine the value and meaning of parent-child relationships. There are two fundamental sets of concerns. The first is that the intrusion of technology, even if well intended, could reduce the child to an artifact, a product of technological design. Parents would become designers rather than progenitors, etching their will to have a certain kind of child into the genetic code of their offspring. A second source of concern is that such interventions would accelerate tendencies to commodify children and evaluate them according to standards of quality control. In the existing market-based system of financing health care, once initiated, the pull of commerce would make it difficult to erect barriers to prevent the wholesale treatment of inheritable genetic modifications as simply one more commodity in the marketplace, a type of commercial service aimed at delivering the product of a desirable baby to the consumer—in this case, the parents.

There are two other reservations about genetic enhancements noted in the religious literature. Many express concerns that an attempt to improve human heredity will lead to a form of eugenics. It seems unlikely that any country will emulate the centralized and compulsory practices of the Nazis to attempt to reengineer its citizens. The real danger, however, is the possible emergence of what has been termed "soft eugenics," or market-based eugenics. This refers to future attempts by individuals to choose what they believe are beneficent eugenic interventions to "perfect" their progeny by "correcting" their genomes so as to conform better to existing social preferences.

The other reservation regards the justice implications of human genetic interventions. Many religious traditions have a commitment to social and economic justice and are concerned about existing inequalities in access to health care. For people of faith, this situation violates the belief that the benefits of creation, including those that come from human effort, are to be wisely shared. This makes many within the religious community particularly sensitive to the issue of equity in access to genetic technologies. Health-insurance policies rarely cover anything considered to be nontherapeutic. This would, of course, apply to genetic enhancement modifications. The likely development of such technologies in the private sector on a for-profit basis means that they will probably be very expensive and thus available only to a narrow, wealthy segment of society. Inheritable genetic modifications also will have a cumulative impact. The likelihood is that people who are now able to afford a range of benefits, such as private schooling had lessons that advantage their children, will also be able to purchase genetic improvements for their children and their children's descendants, thereby increasing their advantages. . . .

Finding New Ground for the Soul

Perhaps the most notable challenge for theologians is drawing the implications of genetic science for understanding the human essence, portrayed in classical theology as the soul or spirit. Genetic research, like work in the neurosciences, makes it difficult to maintain a dualistic conception of a sell that is divided into a body and soul. The findings from genetic science therefore render problematic religious doctrines that describe the soul as completely distinct from the body and consisting of a fundamentally different kind of being. To take genetic science seriously requires an integrated and embodied view of the human person. This has prompted some theologians and ethicists to attempt to reformulate a notion of the human essence that is neither reductionistic [reducible to mere chemistry and physics] nor dualistic.

One promising line of interpretation is the development of a "nonreductive physicalist" account of the person by a multidisciplinary group of scholars in a collection of articles titled *Whatever Happened to the Soul?* The volume reconceptualizes the human soul as a physiologically embodied property of human nature, not a separate entity with a distinctive existence, awareness, and agency. Several of the authors propose an understanding of the soul as a dimension of human experiences that arises out of personal relatedness. According to one of these essays, written by a psychologist, experiences of relatedness to others, to the self, and most particularly to God endow a person with the attributes that traditionally have been attributed to the soul.

A nonreductionist-physicalist approach is consistent with the work of several theologians that defines the human soul as a set of capabilities defined by genes, but not entirely determined by them. Ronald Cole-Turner, for example, suggests thinking of the soul or self as the coherence within the complexity of the human organism, a coherence that is genetically conditioned but also transcends that conditioning. In like manner, Karen Lebacqz offers a view of the soul as a symbol of the covenant between God and each person. For Anne M. Clifford, C.S.J., the soul is synonymous with the center of human individuation. . . .

In Search of Informed Ethics

Developing a scientifically-based prescriptive ethics clearly will require religious thinkers and communities to develop new approaches to dealing with science. A major problem is that it is quite difficult to apply theological reflections developed in pre-scientific cultures to the interpretation and analysis of genetic developments. Sacred texts rarely, if ever, directly address the types of issues raised by genetic advances. Such issues as the fabrication and alteration of microscopic embryos outside the womb from extracted gametes, for example, introduce unique quandaries unimagined in canonical texts. In testimony on the appropriateness of undertaking human cloning, Aziz Sachedina, a Muslim bioethicist at the University of Virginia, pointed out to the (U.S.) National Bioethics Advisory Commission that the Qur'an and the Islamic tradition lack even a universally accepted definition of an embryo. So, too, with other sacred texts and traditions.

The ability of religious thinkers to address cutting-edge scientific and technological issues also requires the development of new ways to apply abstract theological concepts and ethical norms to complex scientific innovations. Many core theological concepts, particularly in the Christian tradition, function like metaphors or symbols. By this I mean that religious affirmations, such as the assertion that humans are created in the image of God, tend to evoke a range of meanings rather than to have a fixed and carefully defined content. This characteristic historically has been an asset because it has enabled religious traditions to adjust and adapt to varying situations without entirely losing their original meaning. This also makes it difficult, however, for these symbols or concepts to serve as standards or criteria by which to evaluate scientific developments and to formulate action guides.

One example is the concept of stewardship, which Christianity shares with Islam and Judaism. This tradition characterizes the vocation of humanity as a servant or vice-regent given the responsibility for management of something belonging to another—in this case, the creator—to manage in trust, consistent with the intentions of the owner. The classical notion of stewardship, however, predates the scientific understanding of evolution and assumes a static, finished, and hierarchically organized universe in which every creature and life-form has its own place. In such a universe, stewardship implies respecting the natural order and not seeking to change it. Twentieth-century science contradicts these assumptions by showing that nature is dynamic and ever evolving. This suggests that it is appropriate for humanity to make at least some changes in the order of things. But, on what basis should we draw a line between what is appropriate for a steward as an exercise of God-given intelligence and creativity, and what constitutes a transgression in a dynamic and ever changing creation? Some of the religious work on genetics utilizes traditional conceptions of stewardship without acknowledging the need for a fundamental rethinking of what stewardship means. A few Christian theologians have begun to address this complex and significant issue, but none has done so in a fully satisfactory manner.

Because theology and ethics are based on sweeping, first-order principles (such as love of neighbor) and abstract concepts (such as human dignity), their interface with science is further complicated. Religious thinkers have traditionally been in dialogue with philosophy. In the process, theologians have developed a capacity to reflect abstractly on such topics as personhood, often at the expense of a capacity to apply these concepts to specific issues. It is one thing to intuit that genetic developments have implications for human dignity, and quite another to evaluate within specific societal contexts the long-term implications that particular technologies have for human dignity. The capacity to address cutting-edge scientific and technological issues raised by genetics therefore requires the development of new ways of applying theological concepts and critical norms to complex scientific innovations. To put the matter another way, theological concepts must be "operationalized," translated into more concrete precepts with clear empirical criteria.

In addition, there is a need to develop ethical norms that can serve as action guides. Most of the current literature presents norms for determining the ethical implications of genetic technologies and applications at a level of abstraction too abstract for direct application. These broad principles or norms need to be further disaggregated or "operationalized" so as to be able to provide the basis for ethical analyses and policy recommendations. This will require the formulation of middle axioms, which have been described as "more concrete than a universal ethical principle and less specific than a program that includes legislation and political strategy. They are the next steps our generation must take in fulfilling the purposes of God." Developing such middle axioms is clearly a task that requires a far clearer and more specific self-understanding of the views and recommendations of religious communities and their individual thinkers. It demands moving beyond generalities to a clear vision based on specifics.

Gene Therapy's Threat to Equality

By Francis Fukuyama

If successful, gene therapy might one day do far more than correct defective genes that lead to terrible diseases. It might lead to enhancements in memory, problem-solving ability, physical strength, and appearance. In the following selection, taken from his book *Our Posthuman Future: Consequences of the Biotechnology Revolution*, political scientist Francis Fukuyama observes that such developments could widen the gap between the haves and have-nots, as affluent people pay to have their children genetically engineered for success. Fukuyama worries that gene therapy could destroy the presumption of equality that makes a democratic society healthy. On the other hand, he notes, it is conceivable that liberal governments may one day require that people in the poorer, less successful segments of society be genetically enhanced to preserve equality. Still, he urges strict regulation and a go-slow approach to gene therapy. Fukuyama is a former State Department official who leaped to prominence in 1989 with a paper in which he declared that the end of the Cold War meant the triumph of liberal democracy everywhere. He now teaches at Johns Hopkins University.

The reasons for the persistence of the idea of the equality of human dignity are complex. Partly it is a matter of the force of habit and what Max Weber once called the "ghost of dead religious beliefs" that continue to haunt us. Partly it is the product of historical accident: the last important political movement to explicitly deny the premise of universal human dignity was Nazism, and the horrifying consequences of the Nazis' racial and eugenic policies were sufficient to inoculate those who experienced them for the next couple of generations.

But another important reason for the persistence of the idea of the universality of human dignity has to do with what we might call the nature of nature itself. Many of the grounds on which certain groups were historically denied their share of human dignity were proven to be simply a matter of prejudice, or else based on cultural and environmental conditions that could be changed. The notions that women were too irrational or emotional to participate in politics, and that immigrants from southern Europe had smaller head sizes and were less intelligent than those from northern Europe, were overturned on the basis of sound, empirical science. That moral order did not completely break down in the West in the wake of the destruction of consensus over traditional religious values should not surprise us either, because moral order comes from within human nature itself and is not something that has to be imposed on human nature by culture.

A Lottery for Everybody

All of this could change under the impact of future biotechnology. The most clear and present danger is that the large genetic variations between individuals will narrow and become clustered within certain distinct social groups. Today, the "genetic lottery" guarantees that the son or daughter of a rich and successful parent will not necessarily inherit the talents and abilities that created conditions conducive to the parent's success. Of course, there has always been a degree of genetic selection: assortative mating means that successful people will tend to marry each other and, to the extent that their success is genetically based, will pass on to their children better life opportunities. But in the future, the full weight of modern technology can be put in the service of optimizing the kinds of genes that are passed on to one's offspring. This means that social elites may not just pass on social advantages but embed them genetically as well. This may one day include not only characteristics like intelligence and beauty, but behavioral traits like diligence, competitiveness, and the like.

The genetic lottery is judged as inherently unfair by many because it condemns certain people to lesser intelligence, or bad looks, or disabilities of one sort or another. But in another sense it is profoundly egalitarian, since everyone, regardless of social class, race, or ethnicity, has to play in it. The wealthiest man can and often does have a good-for-nothing son; hence the saying "Shirtsleeves to shirtsleeves in three generations." When the lottery is replaced by choice, we open up a new avenue along which human beings can compete, one that threatens to increase the disparity between the top and bottom of the social hierarchy.

Threat of a Permanent Aristocracy

What the emergence of a genetic overclass will do to the idea of universal human dignity is something worth pondering. Today, many bright and successful young people believe that they owe their success to accidents of birth and upbringing but for which their lives might have taken a very different course. They feel themselves, in other words, to be lucky, and they are capable of feeling sympathy for people who are less lucky than they. But to the extent that they become "children of choice" who have been genetically selected by their parents for certain characteristics, they may come to believe increasingly that their success is a matter not just of luck but of good choices and planning on the part of their parents, and hence something deserved. They will look, think, act, and perhaps even feel differently from those who were not similarly chosen, and may come in time to think of themselves as different kinds of creatures. They may, in short, feel themselves to be aristocrats, and unlike aristocrats of old, their claim to better birth will be rooted in nature and not convention.

Aristotle's discussion of slavery in Book I of the *Politics* is instructive on this score. It is often condemned as a justification of Greek slavery, but in fact the discussion is far more sophisticated and is relevant to our thinking about genetic classes. Aristotle makes a distinction between conventional and natural slavery. He argues that slavery would be justified by nature if it were the case that there were people with naturally slavish natures. It is not clear from his discussion that he believes such people exist: most actual slavery is conventional—that is, it is the result of victory in war or force, or based on the wrong opinion that barbarians as a class should be slaves of Greeks. The noble-born think their nobility comes from nature rather than acquired virtue and that they can pass it on to their children. But, Aristotle notes, nature is "frequently unable to bring this about." So why not, as Lee Silver suggests, "seize this power" to give children genetic advantages and correct the defect of natural equality?

The Egalitarian Alternative

The possibility that biotechnology will permit the emergence of new genetic classes has been frequently noted and condemned by those who have speculated about the future. But the opposite possibility also seems to be entirely plausible—that there will be an impetus toward a much more genetically egalitarian society. For it seems highly unlikely that people in modern democratic societies will sit around complacently if they see elites embedding their advantages genetically in their children.

Indeed, this is one of the few things in a politics of the future that people are likely to rouse themselves to fight over. By this I mean not just fighting metaphorically, in the sense of shouting matches among talking heads on TV and debates in Congress, but actually picking up guns and bombs and using them on other people. There are very few domestic political issues today in our rich, self-satisfied liberal democracies that can cause people to get terribly upset, but the specter of rising genetic inequality may well get people off their couches and into the streets.

If people get upset enough about genetic inequality, there will be two alternative courses of action. The first and most sensible would simply be to forbid the use of biotechnology to enhance human characteristics and decline to compete in this dimension. But the notion of enhancement may become too powerfully attractive to forgo, or it may prove difficult to enforce a rule preventing people from enhancing their children, or the courts may declare they have a right to do so. At this point a second possibility opens up, which is to use that same technology to raise up the bottom.

This is the only scenario in which it is plausible that we will see a liberal democracy of the future get back into the business of state-sponsored eugenics. The bad old form of eugenics discriminated against the disabled and less intelligent by forbidding them to have children. In the future, it may be possible to breed children who are more intelligent, more healthy, more "normal." Raising the bottom is something that can only be accomplished through the intervention of the state. Genetic enhancement technology is likely to be expensive and involve some risk, but even if it were relatively cheap and safe, people who are poor and lacking in education would still fail to take advantage of it. So the bright red line of universal human dignity will have to be reinforced by allowing the state to make sure that no one falls outside it.

Political Complications

The politics of breeding future human beings will be very complex. Up to now, the Left has on the whole been opposed to cloning, genetic engineering, and similar biotechnologies for a number of reasons, including traditional humanism, environmental concerns, suspicion of technology and of the corporations that produce it, and fear of eugenics. The Left has historically sought to play down the importance of heredity in favor of social factors in explaining human outcomes. For people on the Left to come around and support genetic engineering for the disadvantaged, they would first have to admit that genes are important in determining intelligence and other types of social outcomes in the first place.

The Left has been more hostile to biotechnology in Europe than in North America. Much of this hostility is driven by the stronger environmental movements there, which have led the campaign, for example, against genetically modified foods. (Whether certain forms of radical environmentalism will translate into hostility to human biotechnology remains to be seen. Some environmentalists see themselves defending nature from human beings, and seem to be more concerned with threats to nonhuman than to human nature.) The Germans in particular remain very sensitive to anything that smacks of eugenics. The philosopher Peter Sloterdijk raised a storm of protest in 1999 when he suggested that it will soon be impossible for people to refuse the power of selection that biotechnology provides them, and that the questions of breeding something "beyond" man that were raised by [philosopher Friedrich] Nietzsche and Plato could no longer be ignored. He was condemned by the sociologist Jürgen Habermas, among others, who in other contexts has also come out against human cloning.

On the other hand, there are some on the Left who have begun to make the case for genetic engineering. John Rawls argued in *A Theory of Justice* that the unequal distribution of natural talents was inherently unfair. A Rawlsian should therefore want to make use of biotechnology to equalize life chances by breeding the bottom up, assuming that prudential considerations concerning safety, cost, and the like would be settled. [Legal scholar] Ronald Dworkin has laid out a case for the right of parents to genetically engineer their children based on a broader concern to protect autonomy, and [law professor] Laurence Tribe has suggested that a ban on cloning would be wrong because it might create discrimination against children who were cloned in spite of the ban.

It is impossible to know which of these two radically different scenarios—one of growing genetic inequality, the other of growing genetic equality—is more likely to come to pass. But once the technological possibility for biomedical enhancement is realized, it is hard to see how growing genetic inequality would fail to become one of the chief controversies of twenty-first-century politics.

The Importance of Human Dignity

Denial of the concept of human dignity—that is, of the idea that there is something unique about the human race that entitles every member of the species to a higher moral status than the rest of the natural world—leads us down a very perilous path. We may be compelled ultimately to take this path, but we should do so only with our eyes open. . . .

To avoid following that road, we need to take another look at the notion of human dignity, and ask whether there is a way to defend the concept against its detractors that is fully compatible with modern natural science but that also does justice to the full meaning of humanity specificity. I believe that there is.

Gene Therapy's Contribution Toward Equality

By Gregory Stock

Germ line gene therapy—altering the code that parents pass to their children—presents many moral, legal, and technical challenges, says biophysicist and author Gregory Stock in the following selection. One of the biggest concerns, he acknowledges, is that the wealthy will be able to give their children genetic enhancements unavailable to the common people, which many are concerned will promote inequality. However, Stock argues that attempting to ban the technology will in the long run harm everyone. If germ line gene therapy is banned in Germany, for example, wealthy Germans will simply travel to Brussels where it is legal, Stock points out, leaving poor Germans without access to the technology. Moreover, he points out, gene therapy will likely prove more successful in providing genetic cures for everyone than in engineering "superkids" with exceptional mental and physical prowess. While conceding that the government does have a role to play in assuring that the public is properly informed about gene therapy's risks and potential benefits, Stock says the potential for government abuse in trying to regulate the technology is far greater than the dangers inherent in genetic technology itself. Gregory Stock is director of the UCLA Medical School's program in medicine, technology, and society, and author of the 2002 book *Redesigning Humans: Our Inevitable Genetic Future*.

One of the most challenging possibilities that advances in molecular genetics and reproductive biology will bring is that of "designer babies"—the ability of parents to choose the genetic constitutions of their children. Aside from the moral issues of "playing God" or questions of safety and utility, or whether or not it should be banned, people are concerned about the social impacts of such biotechnology.

Concerns about this science usually gravitate towards two divergent possibilities. People either worry that access to it would be so narrow that it would lead to the creation of a genetic elite—equipped with the best genes and environments that money can buy—or so wide that it would become available to the multitudes, who'd make pathological or at least unwise choices. There is much less discussion of what it might mean if the broad population did gain access to such technology and used it cautiously and intelligently.

But before examining the social impact of wide-scale genetic engineering, let us consider where we are now, and how far in the future we're talking about. First of all, with regard to safety and utility, there is simply not enough data to answer these questions. The response to creating a super elite is complex: while some enthusiasts imagine genetic engineering to be so simple that we'll soon have the facility to order superhuman offspring and rear Spiderman-type clones, the cautious argue that the human genome is too complex to unravel let alone shape. Neither view is helpful. The former is pure science fiction, while the latter is ignoring what is already happening and burying its head in the sand. In reality, the likelihood is that engineering the genetics of embryos, as well as developing current practices such as screening (the procedure which removes single cells from embryos in a Petri dish and runs sophisticated genetic tests to decide which of the embryos to implant for in vitro fertilisation (IVF)), will progress like most other new technologies: while many possibilities will be too complicated to effect, and others will be merely difficult, others will be surprisingly easy.

The speed of progress is hard to judge. If such strong criticisms of genetic screening arc valid and virtually all claims about its potential are currently beyond humanity's reach, do we need to bother considering the technology's social consequences? As most attempts to apply it fail again and again, perhaps the effort will eventually collapse under its own weight, and the idea of designer babies will go down as just another turn-of-the-millennium fantasy. The point is that the social challenges presented by genetic engineering will come not with failure, but with success. And success will be more likely after experimentation and research. Strong opponents of "advanced reproduction" such as Leon Kass, chairman of the President's Council on Bioethics in the US, call for circumspection, not because they're worried that the technology will fail, but that it will succeed, and succeed gloriously. They're concerned that safe, reliable genetic interventions might indeed enable us to make our children smarter, healthier and more talented, and that we would be unable to resist such enhancements. They think that such "progress" would be hollow and that the use—and misuse—of biotech would rend the fabric of our society.

Should we therefore ban such technologies? Perhaps. But what effect would that have? One of the problems is that we (scientists) have in fact far less to say about biotech and its social impact than most bioethicists and regulatory officials care to acknowledge. It is one thing to ban human cloning (that only appeals to a small fringe anyhow), but quite another to ban embryo screening: a procedure which, following its development at Hammersmith Hospital in London more than a decade ago, has spread throughout the world and is in wide medical use to avoid cystic fibrosis and other serious genetic diseases.

With no conclusive evidence of human cloning yet, a ban is largely irrelevant. But embryo screening is important. Screening will challenge society deeply once progress from the US Human Genome Project (HGP)—which aims to discover all human genes to render them accessible for biological study—brings parents more interesting choices than are now available. And if you doubt that couples will use such technology, consider a 1991 international poll by Professor Daryl Macer, the director of the Eubios Ethics Institute in Japan. He found that between 22% and 83% of people from eight countries said that they would perform safe genetic interventions to enhance the mental or physical potentials of their "children-to-be", and that between 62% and 91% said that they would use gene therapy to keep a future child from inheriting even non-fatal diseases such as diabetes.

Given that such technology may soon be feasible in thousands of laboratories throughout the world, the question is not if, but when, where, and how such technology will be used. The legal status of various procedures in different countries may hasten or retard their arrival, but will have little enduring impact, because the genomic and reproductive technologies needed to realise these capabilities are spin-offs of mainstream biomedical research that is moving ahead at breakneck speed.

Indeed, bans will simply drive biotech underground, shift it to other countries and reserve it for the wealthy, who are best positioned to circumvent such restrictions. Germany bans all embryo screening, which simply means that affluent, motivated Germans journey to Brussels or London to screen their embryos. Bans, by their very nature, may diminish problems associated with the broad availability of advanced reproductive technologies, but they will compound those associated with unequal access instead.

But for the sake of discussion, let's assume that parents everywhere can make choices about their children's genes that not only enable them to avoid disease, but to select aspects of temperament and personality—and even to enhance attributes like beauty, talent, athleticism, IQ and longevity. How will the challenges change by having broad, easy access to the technology, rather than reserving it for those committed enough to circumvent restrictions, or wealthy enough to afford hefty prices?

One likely intervention is "genetic enhancement", which could divide humanity into two camps: the enhanced and the unenhanced. But genetic enhancement will not soon be bringing aspiring couples elite athletes, geniuses, and other "superkids". Since elite performance depends on as many environmental factors as it does genetic, and although bringing all of them together in just the right way will not be impossible, it will be much harder than simply rectifying some unhappy cluster of genetic factors that diminishes human potential.

Another intervention, single mutation, can cause metabolic and developmental problems that lead to retardation, early heart disease, faulty vision, or any number of other defects. So, no matter what dimension of human performance we consider, it will almost certainly be far easier to identify—or even sculpt genetically—an embryo that develops into "someone average" than to find the rare combinations that bring about the potentials of superstars. Both interventions, however, are enhancements in the sense that they raise the aptitudes of our offspring above what they might otherwise have been.

Just as embryo screening has hitherto been used mainly to avoid having children afflicted by serious genetic diseases, in the foreseeable future it will be used mainly to avoid having babies predisposed to be (in the view of prospective parents) too slow, too sickly, too small, or perhaps too aggressive. The first overall effect of widely available technology (that allows such choices) is clear: it will narrow the overall diversity of such attributes by eliminating negative traits from the lower end of the social spectrum too. In the long run however, this will diminish the value of special genetic potentials by making them more commonplace.

It is interesting that opposition to such parental activity is generally loudest among the educated and affluent, who decry such evocations of eugenics. But are their children not the ones with the most to lose by opening a genetic bazaar to the masses? It is just as easy for the gifted, lucky winners of the genetic lottery of procreation to extol the virtues of random genetic chance as it is for (on the whole) healthy politicians to insist on caution in our attempts to develop new therapies and treatments for disease. Although their policies are made in the public's name, most of them themselves are not ill or racing against time; so, they perhaps can well afford such caution, as they themselves remain largely unaffected.

The irony of enhancement technology is that if it were readily available to most people, it would not be elitist but egalitarian in its impacts. Indeed, it would serve to offset the self-assortment that occurs so "naturally" in a modern meritocracy. Given that our genes contribute meaningfully to who we are (our talents and potentials) and thus to our success and placement in society, and that people tend to choose their mates from among those they interact with socially, it is clear that as barriers to the movement of talent within society break down, populations will increasingly self-sort according to biologically influenced aptitudes.

The danger of allowing only the wealthy (and presumably discerning) to have access to advanced reproductive technology is not that they would evolve into some sort of master race, but that nature's genetic mistakes would become increasingly limited to the underprivileged. Diseases and deficiencies with strong genetic contributions might even come to be seen as afflictions exclusively of this segment of our population, thereby diminishing the sense that we all share such vulnerabilities.

Use of such reproductive technology, however, ultimately may be less driven by affluence than by philosophy, religion and politics. In Macer's international poll, some 90% of couples in Thailand and India said they'd enhance the physical or mental qualities of a child-to-be, whereas in Germany or France far fewer would make such choices. Indeed, were such technology available to anyone who wanted it, some genetic diminutions might soon be restricted to the children of devout Catholics and philosophers who insisted on the "right to an unaltered genetic constitution" asserted by the Council of Europe in 1991. The core question all future parents may one day face is a simple one: why shouldn't we try to spare our children from the deficiencies that plague us or give them talents that we ourselves did not enjoy? If we could make our baby brighter, or healthier, or more attractive, or a better athlete, or otherwise gifted, or simply keep him or her from being overweight, why wouldn't we?

Once it is appreciated that enhancement technology—by its very nature—will be more useful in diminishing the cruelties and disappointments of life's genetic lottery than in improving upon its luckiest outcomes, the technology may seem far less threatening. And as this occurs, pressure to include the technology in basic healthcare coverage is likely to grow. Usage will shift from the infertile, who are doing IVF anyway and see such screening as an add-on, to the wealthy, who see it as a way of protecting and helping their children, to the population at large.

This pattern of technology adoption—which arises not from direct government regulation but from market forces, political pressures and the learning curve for new technology—is surprisingly well aligned with both individual and societal good. It makes sense that genetic screening would initially be seen only as a supplement to traditional IVF, because IVF, which has to be an essential part of any procedure for screening or altering embryos, is deemed by some to be too unpleasant and costly to undertake for uncertain gains. Only as the utility of comprehensive genetic screening is demonstrated will meaningful numbers of affluent individuals begin to embrace the procedures. Similarly, only as increased usage helps to refine the procedures and lowers the costs will such technology become more widely available.

Affluent "early users" may seek solely to benefit themselves and their children, but they will inadvertently serve as test pilots for humanity as a whole. As eager, relatively thoughtful and well-informed volunteers spending their own money, they will be the ideal group to bring society the information it needs about the real utility of the procedures. A strong argument for this lightly regulated path of technology adoption is its overall safety. Early users uncover subtle potential problems while the technology is young and being employed by relatively small numbers of people. The alternative—blocking early adoption—has the unfortunate consequence of moving such early use out of view and denying us the information it would provide. This will not be an immediate problem, but once technical limitations, cost, risk and other factors slowing acceptance of the technology diminish, and the chance of widespread adoption grows, the lack of any substantial long-term experience will be sorely missed. Paradoxically, the net effect of a policy so cautions that it won't allow early volunteers to bear early risks is to amplify the risk that subtle, long-term problems will afflict large numbers of our children and grandchildren.

So, what is government to do? How should it manage the inevitable—parents' choosing various aspects of their children's genetics? My firm belief is that government should do very little at present, other than trying to ensure that people are not being misled about the risks and potentials of these emerging technologies. The worst course of faction would be to respond to vague present anxieties by passing restrictive legislation about imagined future technologies, because such policies will be difficult to modify and are almost certain to be soon outdated.

One thing we must learn to accept is that however much we discuss these challenging issues, we will never reach a consensus about them. Our attitudes depend too much upon history, culture, politics and religion. Indeed, most projections about the challenges that advances in genetics and reproduction will bring reveal less about future realities than about the author's present hopes and fears.

The biggest problems ahead are almost certainly ones that we do not yet see, so whatever policies we enact should include mechanisms to keep the technology out in the open. To make wise future choices about these reproductive possibilities, we will need to stay informed about their successes and failures, see how they are used and misused, understand the impact they have on families and children. Regulators should deal with actual, rather than imagined problems. They should be mindful of egregious abuses by parents, yet accept that the vast majority of parents are simply trying to do what they see as best for their families, and are better judges about that than any regulatory body. And most of all, we need always to guard against governmental projects hoping to effect some so-called improvement for the human race purchased at the expense of some individuals. The potential for governmental abuse in this realm far outweighs any danger we face from individual parental choices.

We must keep in mind that these powerful reproductive technologies are not like nuclear weapons. Mistakes may bring problems to particular individuals and families, but cannot vaporise millions of innocent bystanders. And there is no urgency here. It will take many years for large numbers of people to embrace these technologies, so we will have ample warning of incipient problems and ample time to develop thoughtful and measured legislative responses if they are needed. Our present blindness to the consequences of these technologies is not particularly unusual. The future is always hidden, and when all is said and done, we are going to have to muddle through for a while to gain the knowledge needed to handle these technologies wisely. The alternative is to pull back in fear and let other braver peoples in other braver lands explore these challenging possibilities. But that would be a huge mistake, because the next frontier is not space, it is our own biology, and the coming exploration will be central to the human future.

CHRONOLOGY

1859

Charles Darwin publishes *On the Origin of Species*, raising awareness of the tendency of offspring to differ from their parents, sometimes with fatal results; however, Darwin has no idea what the mechanism of variation might be.

1866

Gregor Mendel publishes a paper detailing his theory of inheritance, based on observations from more than ten years of carefully breeding peas; though his paper is ignored for years, eventually Mendel will be credited with having identified the units of inheritance, which we call genes.

1889

DNA is chemically isolated and identified as a nuclein, though its function remains unknown.

1900

Genetics becomes a discipline within the academic study of biology as Mendel's works are rediscovered and translated into many languages.

1908

Zoologist Thomas Hunt Morgan begins experiments with fruit flies that will lead to proof that genes are organized into chromosomes and an understanding of sexual inheritance.

1922

Morgan publishes the first gene map, showing the locations of several hundred genes along four chromosomes from a fruit fly.

1935

British scientist J.B.S. Haldane becomes the first to calculate the frequency of spontaneous mutation of a human gene.

1944

O.T. Avery and fellow researchers at Rockefeller University show that DNA is the molecule responsible for inheritance; how it performs this function remains a mystery.

1951

Rosalind Franklin obtains sharp X-ray diffraction photographs of DNA.

1953

Francis Crick and James Watson publish a brief paper explaining the structure of DNA; their discovery clears the way for direct genetic experimentation.

1963

Microbiologist Joshua Lederberg speculates in an article called "The Biological Future of Man" that manipulation of genes may one day become possible.

1966

Lederberg and other scientists for the first time specifically suggest the use of gene therapy to cure disease.

1970

First genetic manipulation experiment takes place, as Stanfield Rogers injects two German sisters suffering from a genetic defect with a virus intended to improve their condition; the experiment is halted before a therapeutic dose can be administered, in part because of controversy over the procedure.

1971

Progress on gene-splicing raises concerns about biohazards; debate among researchers in the field will rage for two years before a formal review mechanism is created.

1972

The first recombinant (gene-spliced) DNA molecules are produced.

1973

The first Recombinant DNA Advisory Committee (RAC) is convened; henceforth, the RAC will play a key role in the design and regulation of genetic experiments.

1974

Scientists establish a voluntary moratorium on recombinant DNA genetic research.

1975

More than one hundred scientists from seventeen countries gather at the Asilomar Conference to consider the risks of recombinant DNA; they call on governments to regulate genetic engineering.

1976

The National Institutes of Health publish their first recombinant DNA research guidelines.

1977

Protesters, concerned about the possibility of a genetically engineered superbug being released into the environment, demonstrate at a National Academy of Sciences symposium.

1980

Three major religious organizations—the National Council of Churches, the Synagogue Council of America, and the United States Catholic Conference—publish a letter to President Jimmy Carter expressing concern about scientists playing God with genetic engineering.

1985

A team of researchers led by W. French Anderson successfully demonstrates the use of retroviruses to carry corrective genes into human cells in a lab dish experiment.

1988

The Human Genome Project sets out to map the entire sequence of human DNA.

1989

A human gene is transferred into a human patient for the first time in an attempt to track tumor-infiltrating lymphocytes injected into the patient to stave off a virulent cancer.

1990

The first full-fledged gene therapy experiment takes place when a four-year-old girl has genetically defective cells removed from her body; they are treated with corrective genes and then reinjected into her body; the treatment continues for two years, with apparent success.

1993

Researchers employ gene therapy to treat babies with the immune disorder ADA deficiency; genes to correct the condition are inserted into blood cells isolated from the babies' umbilical cords.

1998

More than three hundred gene therapy trials are underway around the world.

1999

Jesse Gelsinger, a healthy volunteer in a gene therapy trial at the University of Pennsylvania, dies after a buildup in his body of the viruses intended to convey genes leads to a catastrophic immune response; he is just eighteen at the time of his death.

2000

The Human Genome Project announces preliminary results, including the startling finding that humans have only about thirty thousand active genes, far fewer than had been expected.

2002

France halts gene therapy for children born with immune system deficiencies after two seemingly cured children develop leukemia.

2003

In the wake of France's experience, the U.S. Food and Drug Administration suspends many gene therapy trials that use a retrovirus as vectors; calls for a reevaluation of gene therapy abound; researchers at the University of California, Los Angeles, succeed in transporting genes across the brain's protective barrier using a novel vector; hopes of treating Parkinson's disease rise accordingly; progress in nonviral vectors continues, as scientists focus on tiny fatty molecules called liposomes as transport vehicles for corrective genes.

FOR FURTHER RESEARCH

Books

Allen Buchanan et al., *From Chance to Choice: Genetics and Justice.* New York and Cambridge: Cambridge University Press, 2000.

Carl Cranor, ed., *Are Genes Us? Social Consequences of the New Genetics.* New Brunswick, NJ: Rutgers University Press, 1994.

Editors of Scientific American, *Understanding the Genome.* New York: Warner Books, 2002.

Jeff Lyon and Peter Gorner, *Altered Fates: Gene Therapy and the Retooling of Human Life.* New York: W.W. Norton, 1995.

Eric C. Reeve, ed., *The Encyclopedia of Genetics.* Philadelphia: Taylor & Francis, 2000.

Matt Ridley, *Genome: The Autobiography of a Species in Twenty-Three Chapters.* New York: HarperCollins, 2000.

Jeremy Rifkin, *The Biotech Century: Harnessing the Gene and Remaking the World.* Los Angeles: J.P. Tarcher, 1998.

Jeremy Rifkin and Ted Howard, *Who Should Play God?* New York: Dell, 1977.

Gregory Stock, *Redesigning Humans: Our Inevitable Genetic Future.* New York: Houghton Mifflin, 2002.

Gregory Stock and John Campbell, eds., *Engineering the Human Germline: An Exploration of the Science and Ethics of Altering the Genes We Pass to Our Children.* New York: Oxford University Press, 2000.

R.G. Vile and N.R. Lemoine, *Understanding Gene Therapy.* Oxford: BIOS Scientific, 1998.

Mark Walker and David McKay, *Unravelling Genes: A Layper-*

son's Guide to Genetic Engineering. Crow's Nest, Australia: Allen & Unwin, 2000.

Richard Walker and Catherine Brereton, eds., *Genes and DNA.* New York: Houghton Mifflin, 2003.

Periodicals

W. French Anderson, "Genetic Engineering and Our Humanness," *Human Gene Therapy*, June 1994.

W. French Anderson, "Human Gene Therapy," *Science*, May 8, 1992.

Natalie Angier, "For First Time, Gene Therapy Is Tested on Cancer Patients," *New York Times*, January 30, 1991.

Geoffrey Baskerville, "Human Gene Therapy: Application, Ethics, and Regulation," *Dickinson Law Review*, Summer 1992.

David Bekelman, "Human Germ-Line Gene Therapy: New Territory?" *Pharos*, Fall 1993.

David M. Danks, "Germ-Line Gene Therapy: No Place in Treatment of Genetic Disease," *Human Gene Therapy*, February 1994.

Robert Elliot, "Identity and the Ethics of Gene Therapy" *Bioethics*, January 1993.

John Harris, "Is Gene Therapy a Form of Eugenics?" *Bioethics*, April 1993.

Joel D. Howell, "The History of Eugenics and the Future of Gene Therapy," *Journal of Clinical Ethics*, Winter 1991.

Eliot Marshall, "Gene Therapy Worries Grow," *ScienceNOW*, January 14, 2003.

Rosie Mestel, "Gene Therapy Undergoes a Reevaluation," *Los Angeles Times*, November 12, 2002.

Abbey S. Meyers, "Gene Therapy and Genetic Diseases: Revisiting the Promise," *Human Gene Therapy*, October 1994.

David Resnik, "Debunking the Slippery Slope Argument Against Human Germ-Line Gene Therapy," *Journal of Medicine and Philosophy*, February 1994.

Eugene Russo, "Reconsidering Asilomar," *Scientist*, April 3, 2000.

Larry Thompson, "Human Gene Therapy: Harsh Lessons, High Hopes," *FDA Consumer*, September/October 2000, www.fda. gov.

Nicholas Wade, "Searching for Genes to Slow the Hands of Biological Time," *New York Times*, September 26, 2000.

LeRoy Walters, "Ethical Issues in Human Gene Therapy," *Journal of Clinical Ethics*, Winter 1991.

Web Sites

Access Excellence at the National Health Museum, www. accessexcellence.org. Access Excellence is a national educational program that provides critical sources of new scientific information on the World Wide Web. Its Web site offers scientific updates, information about biotechnology, activities, and a special section just for students.

DOEgenomes.org, www.ornl.gov. The DOEgenomes.org Web site is maintained by the U.S. Department of Energy Office of Science, the founder of the Human Genome Project and leader in systems biology research. The Web site offers information about the Human Genome Project (HGP) and the Genomes to Life Project, a follow-up to the HGP that explores how genes and DNA function to create living systems.

The Web site of W. French Anderson, www.frenchanderson.org. The Web site of W. French Anderson, the father of gene therapy, offers biographical information about the doctor, a history of gene therapy, updates on the latest gene therapy trials, and articles about the ethics of gene therapy technology.

INDEX